248

POSITIVE CHRISTIAN LIVING

J. J. Turner

Thanks very much for everything Karen

Copyright 1983 by J. J. Turner

Revised

```
D1563684
```

QUALITY PUBLICATIONS
P.O. BOX 1060
ABILENE, TEXAS 79604

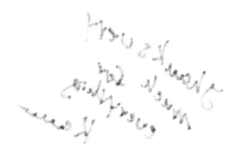

DEDICATION

To

LARRY AND PEGGY WEST

They have been a special source of encouragement to
me during times when it was difficult to be positive.

ISBN:0-89137-316-0

TABLE OF CONTENTS

INTRODUCTION

When a person becomes a Christian he moves from a negative way of life to a positive way of life. Jesus made it very clear that He came so that we "may have LIFE and have it more abundantly" (cf. John 10:10). This is not speculation, but a divine promise. As a child of the King life now has meaning and purpose. From beginning to end (i. e. initial salvation to the heavenly home), Christianity centers in a positive Savior, based on a positive hope, revealed in a positive message, and encourages to positive attitudes and actions.

While all these facts are true about the positive nature of Christianity, it doesn't automatically mean, however, that every Christian is living a dynamic, positive Christian life. This is evidenced by the tide of negativism in our midst.

Have you noticed how quickly many Christians in their conversations get around to the negatives? To listen to some Christians talk you would think that God has commanded "Thou shalt be pessimistic" in His word.

How sad for members of the King's family to live as though they are paupers. Tragic indeed is the son of God who walks around like "Sad Sack," with one negative remark after another falling from his lips. You would never guess that he has a joy unspeakable and a peace that passeth all understanding promised to him by God. The point is this: he has never accepted it as a reality in his life.

Someone has said, "Many Christians have just enough Christianity to be miserable." We must realize, however, it is not that Christianity fails, but the Christian. The system is good. Man is the weak link! It's an insult to the Great Emancipator for free men (cf. John 8:36) to walk about in the chains of self-bondage. A bondage of fear, worry and negativism.

I want to challenge YOU to do something about all this "sour pickle" Christianity. The key is to become a positive Christian in your daily living. This is one step beyond a positive spiritual attitude. This is ACTION.

For a number of years I have been convinced that we will never make any great advancements in the Lord's work until a change occurs in the attitudes of many Christians. We must change attitudes before we can change lives.

In this book I have set forth some core truths that are designed to help you move ahead in daily positive Christian living. The material in this book has been used effectively in positive spiritual attitude seminars across the nation. It has helped people change their lives in a positive way. It will help you too. The challenge is to use it. NOW!

Remember this truth as you read and study this material. You may not be able to change the world but you can change yourself; after all, a better world begins with YOU.

J. J. Turner, D. Min.
Garden Grove, California

TIPS FOR USING THIS BOOK IN CLASS STUDY

This book is designed to be studied. It may be studied on a personal basis or in a class situation. If you plan to use it in a class situation, I would suggest the following things to help you have the best possible class.

1. Be sure each member of the class has a copy of this book.
2. Encourage each member to read and study a chapter before you cover it in class.
3. As the teacher find some good illustrations for some of the major points in each lesson. Encourage each member of the class to do likewise.
4. Teach the material in your own words.
5. Go over the "For Thought and Discussion" section in class. Encourage members of the class to bring written answers to class.
6. Prepare your own set of questions over the material, etc.
7. Allow the class time to discuss major points.
8. Be sure to encourage personal application of the material before you leave each class.
9. You may begin each class by asking the members to share how they have used the material studies in the last class (during the week).
10. Find additional verses of scripture for the lesson.
11. If time permits allow group work. (e.g., Getting into smaller groups for discussion and application, etc.: "Here is how I can use this point"; "Here is what this means to me.").
12. Be creative.
13. Recommend reading in other books on certain subjects covered in a lesson.
14. Pray for wisdom (cf. James 1:5).

CHAPTER ONE

POSITIVE CHRISTIAN LIVING

"Why are Christians so miserable and negative?" How would you answer this question asked by a skeptic? Do you agree with it? Why? Why not? Have you ever met a negative Christian? Sure you have!

Nothing has done more to turn people away from Christianity than the negative attitudes of many Christians. "Why should I leave my happy life to become part of those unhappy people in the church?" How applicable is this question to the congregation you are a member of? Are you a positive Christian?

It has been estimated that 4 out of 10 Christians aren't sure they have eternal life. This is saying that 40% of us aren't living a full, positive life for the Lord. Many are *saved* but still remain *slaves* to their old way of life. They aren't enjoying all the spiritual blessings that are in Christ (cf. Ephesians 1:3). Jesus said, "I am come that ye might have life and have it more abundantly" (John 10:36). Thus, "If the Son shall make you free, you shall be free indeed" (John 8:36). Many are living in self-bondage even though they are free in Christ. This is sad!

What comes to your mind when you think of positive Christian living? Whom do you think of when you think of positive Christian living? How would you define positive Christian living?

Positive: _____

Christian: _____

Living: _____

QUALITIES OF POSITIVE CHRISTIAN LIVING

1. Positive Christian living begins with a denial of self (cf. Matthew 16:24). This means crucifixion of the old man. This is hard to do, but do it we must.

2. Positive Christian living centers in knowing God. Jesus said, "This is eternal life, that they might know thee the only true God, and Jesus Christ, whom thou has sent" (John 17:3). Paul said, "I know in whom I believeth." This essential knowledge comes only through studying the Bible (cf. II Timothy 2:15).

3. Positive Christian living means total commitment to Christ as Lord of your life. The Master asked, "And why call ye me, Lord, Lord, and do not the things which I say?" (Luke 6:46). This means that nothing or no one comes between you and the Lord.

4. Positive Christian living has the goal of growing into the fullness of Christ. Paul wrote: "Till we all come in the unity of the faith, and of the knowledge of the Son of God, unto a perfect man, unto the measure of the stature of the fullness of Christ" (Ephesians 4:13).

5. Positive Christian living involves serving God in every situation: Be not conformed to this world: but be ye transformed by the renewing of your mind, that ye may prove what is that good, and acceptable, and perfect, will of God" (Romans 12:2).

6. Positive Christian living is believing that all things work together for good (cf. Romans 8:28). This doesn't mean that all things may be good in and of themselves, but God is able to bring good out of it for our benefit.

7. Positive Christian living is possible through trusting God's power (cf. Ephesians 3:20). You can't do it by yourself.

8. Positive Christian living is seen by others. They take knowledge of you that you have been with Jesus (cf. Acts 4:13). This involves letting our light shine before others.

9. Positive Christian living is demonstrated in love for everybody, even one's enemies (cf. Matthew 5:44). The qualities of this love is seen in I Corinthians 13.

10. Positive Christian living involves being an active, productive member of the Body of Christ (cf. I Corinthians 12:12-28). Each member seeks to find and fulfill his

ministry in the church (cf. Ephesians 4:11-13).

11. Positive Christian living centers in positive thoughts. The wise man said, "As a man thinketh in his heart, so is he" (Proverbs 23:7). Negative Christian living results from negative thoughts.

12. Positive Christian living depends upon God's word for direction: "Thy word is a lamp unto my feet, and a light unto my path." (Psalm 119:97). It is not in man that walketh to direct his steps.

13. Positive Christian living continues through death (cf. Revelation 2:10). It is not a one time thing, but must continue every day of our lives.

14. Positive Christian living is shared with others. This is the spirit of Christianity (cf. Mark 16:15, 16). We must go and tell others about the hope we have in Christ.

Positive Christian living is a step beyond positive spiritual thinking. It is a life-style. It is doing.

REWARDS OF POSITIVE CHRISTIAN LIVING

There are many reasons why a person should desire a life that is lived for God in a positive manner. The rewards of such a life are many. Some of the major rewards are as follows:

1. It helps a person be pleasing unto the Lord. This is the goal of every Christian. Negative living is contrary to God's desire for us.

2. Positive Christian living brings happiness and peace of mind (cf. Matthew 5:1-8).

3. A joy unspeakable is another reward of living a positive Christian life (cf. I Peter 1:8).

4. It helps you defeat the devil (cf. James 4:7; Ephesians 6:11-18).

5. It helps you produce the fruit of the spirit in your life (cf. Galatians 5:22-26).

6. It glorifies God (cf. Revelation 4:11).

7. It brings the crown of life in the end (cf. Revelation 2:10).

HOW TO DEVELOP A POSITIVE CHRISTIAN LIFE

The following things will help you develop a positive Christian life. Study each one very carefully.

1. You must resolve in your heart that you want to live a positive Christian life. Will you do this?

2. You must develop a plan to daily renew your mind (cf. Ephesians 4:23). The old mind is enmity against God (cf. Colossians 1:21).

3. A positive Christian life results from a daily meditating in God's word (cf. Psalm 119:97-105). This is our source of direction.

4. Set spiritual goals and work on them on a daily basis. You should also set goals for every area of your life.

5. Pray for wisdom to know how to conduct yourself as a positive Christian (cf. James 1:5).

6. Associate with positive Christians (cf. I Corinthians 15:33). Nothing makes you negative quicker than being around negative persons.

7. Do daily works of faith (cf. James 2).

8. Don't quit! This is the major reason why most persons don't live a positive Christian life–they get discouraged and quit. You must finish the race.

WHAT WE HAVE TO BE POSITIVE ABOUT

1. Our God is alive (Genesis 1-2-3).
2. Our Saviour (Matthew 1:21; Revelation 1:5).
3. Our Bible (II Timothy 3:16, 17).
4. Our Salvation (I John 5:13).
5. Our Power (Ephesians 3:20).
6. Our Reward (Revelation 2:10).
7. The Church (Matthew 16:13-18).
8. Our Hope (Romans 8:24).

FOR THOUGHT AND DISCUSSION

1. Why do negative Christians do harm to the church?

2. What is YOUR definition of positive Christian living?

3. On a scale of 1 to 10 how would you rate your positive Christian living attitude?

4. Discuss the meaning of I John 5:13 and how it relates to positive Christian living.

5. Who is the most positive living Christian person you know? Why?

6. How can the church promote positive Christian living? Discuss a possible plan.

7. What are some major enemies to positive Christian living?

8. Share two Bible verses on positive Christian living.

9. List three ways this lesson has helped you.

10. List three applications you plan to make of this lesson.

CHAPTER TWO

YOU ARE RESPONSIBLE FOR YOUR LIFE

A mother stood before the judge with tears in her eyes, and said, "Your Honor, Harold is not responsible for all those horrible things they said he did. Those bums he has been running around with are to blame."

An angry mother shouted at the high school teacher, "You're the reason why Mary isn't passing in school."

A young boy tells his mother, after she scolds him for coming home late, "Well, the others wouldn't let me leave until the game was over."

A man fresh from divorce court spends his time telling anyone who will listen how his wife is responsible for the fact that he ran around with other women.

A church member has stopped attending church services. Upon being visited, she says, "The members of the church are snobs. They drove me away with their lack of friendliness."

A middle-age man curses his boss because he isn't given a raise. His favorite line is, "The boss just doesn't like me."

An overweight husband justifies his problem by saying, "If my wife wouldn't insist that I have a second and third helping, I wouldn't have this weight problem. I don't want to offend her."

What do these seven illustrations have in common? They all illustrate the *blame game* humans so frequently and easily play. There is rarely a day which passes that we don't come in contact with players of this game. Most of us are prone to practice it ourselves.

If you hope to develop a positive Christian life-style, you must become a totally responsible person. You must accept the responsibility for your life. You must be willing to accept the blame for your faults, failures, weaknesses, mistakes, etc. When you shift the blame to others, you are still responsible. This is a truth which many persons never seem to learn.

"Whom shall I blame?" is the perpetual question in the mind of the person who doesn't want to accept responsibility for his life and actions. Someone has said, "There is only one thing you are not responsible for — your birth." I believe this is especially true morally and spiritually. The great challenge, therefore, is to accept responsibility for your life.

THE BIBLE AND RESPONSIBILITY

The blame game is played in every area of human endeavor. The social worker blames the community; the psychologist blames the parents; the dietitian blames the food manufactors; the speeder blames the policeman; the loser blames luck; the pessimist blames fate; the Christian blames God; the sinner blames the devil; and on and on it goes. We have developed an attitude which demands a shifting of responsibility from self to someone else.

In the midst of all this blaming, God's word speaks loudly and clearly. Man is responsible for his actions! More specifically, YOU are responsible for your life and actions; I am responsible for my life and actions. *Accountability* is the key word. The most frightening fact we have to face is that: ". . .every one of us shall give account of HIMSELF to God" (Romans 14:12).

The first Bible account of the blame game is the case of Adam and Eve. After God created them, He placed them under positive, divine law which specifically revealed their freedom of choice. They had the choice to freely eat of every tree but one (cf. Genesis 1, 2, 3). Eve, however, chose to obey the voice of Satan rather than God (cf. Genesis 3:1-10).

Adam quickly followed the example of his wife and violated God's commandment (cf. Genesis 3:6). Soon after their sin, God calls them into account. "And the man said, "The woman whom thou gavest to be with me, she gave me of the tree, and I did eat" (Genesis 3:12). Adam blames Eve for his sin. When God talks to Eve about the transgression, she said, ". . .The serpent beguiled me, and I did eat" (Genesis 3:13). Eve blames the devil for her sin. Notice God's response to Adam and Eve's attempt to blame others for their actions (cf. Genesis 3:14-24): they are driven from the garden by Him. Thus, from this time onward, it is

13

clearly seen in the Bible that each person is responsible for his own actions.

Another good example of man's responsibility, and how he must answer for what he does, is the provision in the law of Moses which tied blessings and cursings to man's obedience (cf. Deuteronomy 28, 29, 30).

Ezekiel, the prophet of God, stated man's responsibility for his own actions in these words, "The soul that sinneth, it shall die. The son shall not bear iniquity of the father, neither shall the father bear the iniquity of the son: the righteousness of the righteous shall be upon him, and the wickedness of the wicked shall be upon him" (Ezekiel 18:20).

Joshua, a faithful leader for God, made it very clear that each person has the responsibility of choosing whom he will serve (cf. Joshua 24:15).

Jesus makes it very clear that each person will be judged by their response to His words (cf. John 12:48; II Thessalonians 1:7-9). If a person dies lost, he is responsible. James said that each man is responsible for his OWN sins (cf. James 1:17-19). This is why Jesus commanded that the gospel be preached to EVERY creature (cf. Mark 16:15): every creature is responsible for his own sins.

The final judgment is a major key in knowing that God holds the individual responsible for his life: ". . .we shall all stand before the judgment seat of Christ. For it is written, As I live, saith the Lord, every knee shall bow to me, and every tongue shall confess to God. So then EVERY ONE OF US shall give account of HIMSELF to God" (Romans 14:10-12).

It should also be noted that Christian growth is the responsibility of the individual. Peter said, "And beside this, giving all diligence, add to YOUR faith virtue; and to virtue knowledge" (II Peter 1:5). I am responsible for my growth in Christ Jesus (cf. Ephesians 4:12-16). I am presently where I am because of what I have done prior to this point.

Why would God give us commandments if He isn't going to hold us responsible for obeying them? (cf Hebrews 5:8, 9). The Bible teaches that YOU are responsible for your thoughts and actions. Others may provide the entrapment or suggestion to sin, but I am in control of my acceptance or rejection.

WHY BLAME GAME?

There is no way to determine why every person blames someone else for his problems, actions and failures. I do believe, however, that some of the reasons are as follows:

1. It is what you have been exposed to all of your life. Man has the habit of doing what he sees others do.

2. It is the result of fear. Some may not like the consequences of accepting responsibility.

3. It is a weakness of the flesh. This results from a lack of spiritual growth (cf. Galatians 5:19-21).

4. It may be an attempt to escape guilt.

5. A poor self-image may cause a person to reject his responsibility.

6. A lack of courage is a major cause of rejecting responsibility.

7. Ignorance of God's plan for man is another major cause.

8. It is the easy way out. This appeals to the lazy person.

9. It comes from a lack of self-control.

10. It is an evasive tactic for passing the buck to someone else.

11. It comes from a sense of psudo-self-satisfaction, i.e., "I'm not responsible for what happened."

12. It is an act of selfishness.

13. It comes from a sense of wanting to be perfect.

14. A lack of love for self and others may produce a shifting of responsibility.

15. Immaturity causes a person to blame others for his actions.

GETTING SPECIFIC

Normally when a person assumes a new job or responsibility, one of the first things he learns is what it takes to fulfill the job. He will usually ask, "What am I responsible for?" More important, however, than job responsibilities, are the responsibilities of life. YOU are responsible for the things that daily challenge your life. No I don't mean that YOU cause everything that happens. I mean you are responsible for HOW you handle them. You are responsible for the following things (these specific examples will help illustrate my point).

1. You are responsible for what you think (Proverbs 23:7). You have control over what you put into your mind (Philippians 4:7-9).

2. You are responsible for what you say (cf. James 1:19).

3. You are responsible for your actions (cf. James 1:19-23).

4. You are responsible for your feelings.

5. If you don't like yourself, you are responsible.

6. If you don't have friends, you are responsible.

7. If you don't like your job, you are responsible.

8. If you aren't making good grades, you are responsible.

9. If you don't enjoy going to church services, you are responsible.

10. When people are hurt by your association with you, you are responsible.

11. If you are having marriage problems, you are responsible.

12. If you aren't growing as a Christian, you are responsible.

13. If you are not a positive Christian, you are responsible.

14. If you don't like the way you are treated, you are responsible.

15. When you tell someone else to do it, you are responsible.

16. If there are things in your life you don't like, you are responsible.

17. If you don't have enough money, you are responsible.

18. If you aren't happy, you are responsible.

19. If you can't get along with people, you are responsible.

20. When something you have said is passed on, you are responsible.

21. If you lack peace of mind, you are responsible.

22. If you are worrying, you are responsible.

23. When you do what you DON'T want to do, you are responsible.

24. When you say yes when you want to say no, you are responsible.

25. If you are not appreciated, you are responsible.

You will never be happy until you take responsibility for your life. Having done this, turn it over to God and let Him guide you to peace and happiness. Through accepting responsibility for your life you will be able to develop a positive Christian life. It is time for the blame game to end. The closing gun is in your hand. Will you stop the game?

FOR THOUGHT AND DISCUSSION

1. Can you think of an illustration of a person trying to shift the blame to another? Discuss it.

2. Why do children blame others so easily?

3. How does the "blame game" affect the church?

4. Can you think of another Bible example of shifting the blame?

5. What would you say to a person who blames another for his being lost?

6. Name some frequent phrases you hear persons utter as they try to blame God for certain things in their life.

7. How does the "blame game" hurt marriages?

8. Share a personal plan for growing in this area.

9. How have you seen other persons handle responsibility in a positive way?

10. How do you plan to use the material in this lesson?

CHAPTER THREE

BEING THE BEST FOR GOD

I will never forget the occasion or the day. My son had received among his many toys for Christmas, a plastic model car. It must have had a "thousand" pieces to glue together. As I watched his eager young hands quickly open the box and separate the parts, I couldn't help but wonder if he would be able to complete the model which was obviously designed for older children.

I watched and helped him for about an hour glue the larger pieces together, and then left him on his own to continue the job. I wanted it to be his car.

About thirty minutes later I returned and found a very frustrated little boy. I asked him what was wrong.

"I can't do it! It just won't stay together."

"Don't worry about it, son," I replied, "just do the best you can do." I helped him for a few minutes and left him on his own again.

When I returned the second time to see how he was doing, I found an odd looking car. "Son," I said, "what in the world have you done to the car?"

With tears coming into his eyes, he said, "Well, Dad, I'm just doing the best I can do, just like you told me to do."

He had detected in his young sensitive ears a sound of disapproval in my voice. This broke his heart because he was doing the best he could do. I hadn't disapproved his actions, but my unguarded reaction caused him to think so.

I learned a great lesson on that occasion. When someone does his best, especially after you have encouraged him to do so, that's all he can do. Accept it without a rebuke or question. A person's best is always good enough!

Nothing is more frustrating than being rejected or being made fun of because your best is not good enough. Sadly, some persons never learn the truth about doing their best. This is why this subject must be studied.

There are TWO extremes in this matter of doing the best you can do. One is the lazy, do-nothing, just-get-by attitude. The other is a legalistic concept which works for God's approval. Both are frustrating and wrong. Both hinder positive Christian living.

The Bible condemns laziness and undisciplined living. It also points out that deeds done to earn God's favor are "as but filthy rags" (Isaiah 64:6). "When we have done all this we are still unprofitable servants" (Luke 17:10).

"I have done my best for him but it is not enough." These words were spoken by a woman who had left her husband.

"I did my best on the test and still got a C." These words were spoken by a high school student who was thinking about quitting school.

"I just can't be perfect!" This statement was uttered by a new Christian who had left the church.

Everyone has had the experience of feeling like his best was not enough. I have had it, and I know you have had it. Yet, the challenge is still before us to be the best we can be for the Lord. How is this possible?

Here is the good news! Jesus Christ makes you the BEST through His blood and imputed righteousness (cf. Revelation 1:5; Romans 4). The challenge we face daily, however, is to faithfully live our lives in subjection to His will; to mold our minds into His mind (cf. Philippians 2:5-8); and to be the best possible servants we can be for our Master. We must try to live in harmony with what He has made us -- the best! It is in this context that we should want to be and do the best for God. Not for salvation, but because of salvation. This is what positive Christian living is all about: doing our best.

Do you ALWAYS do your best? Somewhere, at some time in your life, someone told you, as you faced a difficult or new situation, "Just do your best." And no doubt, you found courage in the words. This is what God wants you to do -- JUST DO YOUR BEST! Will you try? ( ) yes ( )no

WHY SOME DON'T DO THEIR BEST

Someone has said, "More people would do their best if they had to put their names on the products they have produced." In God's economy this is just what happens.

You must give an account for the deeds done in the body (Romans 14:12). This is an incentive for doing your best.

Many Christians, however, do not do their best. Why? This is a very important question. To which there are several answers.

1. *Some have the habit of laziness.* They are like the man described in the book of Proverbs who was so lazy that he had to be fed (cf. Proverbs 19:24). This is a hard habit to break.

2. *Some have developed a quitters spirit.* They have developed a pattern of never finishing anything they start.

3. *A few are content to live mediocre lives.* They have no interest in being the best at anything. The church is no exception.

4. *Some may not know that they should do their* best for the Lord and the church. They just haven't been taught.

5. *Some don't know HOW to do* any better than they are doing. They just continue doing what they have always been doing.

6. *Some have left their first love* (Revelation 2:4). They are just serving God out of rote habit.

7. *Some lack courage to do their best.* They don't want to face "digs" or cutting remarks about their spiritual efforts.

8. *Some really believe they should just do* enough to get by. This is a popular standard.

9. *Some aren't properly taught in the word.*

10. *Some are victims of a "just-get-by" society.*

11. *Some aren't really sold on the importance of God's work.*

12. *Some aren't willing to put forth the effort to do any better.*

Can you think of additional reasons why persons don't do their best?

WHY DO YOUR BEST?

"Why should I try to do my best? No one else is doing his best or even cares." How would you answer this person who was encouraged to do his best?

Anytime we say a person *ought* to do a thing, there should be some good reasons for such an admonition. The following points stress why we should be the best for our heavenly Father.

1. That's all you can do. God hasn't called on you to be more than you can be or do more than you can do. Just do your best!

2. Because of the alternative to not doing your best is doing your worst. This is obviously not desirable. "Whatsoever thy hands find to do, do it with all thy might" (Ecclesiastes 9:10). This proves that God expects our best.

3. Because of the results of not doing your best. It places a stumbling block in front of others.

4. Because a lost world deserves to see the best life we can live for the Lord. We must let our lights shine before men so they will glorify our Father which is in heaven (cf. Matthew 5:16).

5. Because we are created in God's image (cf. Genesis 1:26, 27). This places a unique responsibility upon our shoulders.

6. Because of competition. Denominationalism is, in some cases, doing things that "shame" us because of our lack of effort. God's cause deserves the best.

7. Because of positive results. People will take knowledge that you have been with Jesus (cf. Acts 4:13).

8. Because you will develop good habits from being the best for the Lord.

9. Because the church deserves the best effort you can put forth (I Corinthians 12:12-30).

10. It brings happiness and peace of mind. There is a good feeling in knowing you have done your best for the Lord.

11. Because it will influence others to go and do likewise.

21

1. Resolve, with God's help, to do your best. Say, "I will always do my best for the Lord." Make this resolve every day.

2. Develop a plan for doing your best. It won't just happen.

3. Know that sometimes, try as you may, you will fail to do your best (cf. Romans 7:15-25). Don't let this discourage you or lead you to give up.

4. Pray for wisdom in every situation you face (cf. James 1:5). God has promised to give you help and wisdom.

5. Do all that you do from the heart fervently. Don't be half-hearted.

6. Remember that God is more interested in your *faithfulness* than your success or failures. (cf. Revelation 2:10).

7. Study God's word for guidance and strength (cf. Psalm 119:97-105).

8. Try, try, try and try again. Don't quit.

9. Examine yourself at the end of the day, and ask yourself, "Have I done my best in every situation?" Remember tomorrow is a new day.

10. Be an encourager of others. Help them do their best too.

11. Learn what a job requires and then prepare yourself for it.

12. Remember Jesus. He was the best in every situation. Study His life.

13. Develop a positive spiritual attitude (cf. Ephesians 3:20).

14. Just do it!

APPLICATIONS

Before I conclude this chapter, let me give some examples by way of application of areas we should strive to be the best in for the Lord.

1. Be the best example you can be (cf. I Timothy 4:12).

2. Be the best in love (cf. John 13:35).

3. Be the best forgiver you can possibly be (cf. Luke 17:1-4).

4. Be the best steward with your possessions (cf. Acts 5:4).

5. Be the best in your daily prayer life (I Thessalonians 5:17).

6. Be the best student you can be for the Lord (II Timothy 2:15).

7. Be the best optimist you can be (cf. Romans 8:28).

8. Be the best friend you can be (cf. Proverbs 17:17).

9. Be the best mate you can be to your marriage partner.

10. Be the best servant you can be.

11. Be the best in your attitude toward all things good, etc.

12. Be the best soul winner you can be for the Lord.

13. Be the best at encouraging the brethren.

14. Be the best at everything you do for the Lord.

15. Be the best in every trial that comes upon you (cf. James 1:2-7).

16. Be the best employee or employer (Ephesians 6:5-9).

Under the Law of Moses the best was required of Israel as they offered their sacrifices to the Lord (cf. Book of Leviticus). Today, we must present our best to God, too. Our best is ourselves (cf. Romans 12:1, 2). A self that is totally committed to God and His work.

Positive Christian living centers in being the best you can be for the Lord. Why not the best?

FOR THOUGHT AND DISCUSSION

1. Have you ever heard the expression, "Your best is not good enough"?

2. Have you ever felt like your best wasn't good enough?

3. How does being a "perfectionist" relate to being the best?

4. Share an example of a person, who with limited ability, does his best.

5. What is a major discouragement to persons who try to do their best?

6. How can we help children do their best?

7. Discuss some areas that your congregation can do better in.

8. What would you tell a person who is always just trying to get by with as little as possible?

9. Share some additional verses that relate to being the best for God.

10. How do you plan to use this lesson?

CHAPTER FOUR

GROWING THROUGH GOALS

A man called a local travel agent and told him that he wanted to take a trip out West.

"Where, out West?" asked the agent.

"Oh, just anywhere will do," the man replied.

"But sir," said the frustrated agent, "I need more specifics before I can arrange an itinerary for you. There are hundreds of cities out West."

Most persons go through life like this would-be traveler. They have a vague idea of where they want to go, or what they want to do, but they don't have any specific goals or plans for getting there. This is why many persons never get beyond nominal living. A person will never accomplish much without goals.

Many Christians speak in generalities when they discuss their objectives in life: "I want to go to heaven"; "I want to be more spiritual"; or "I want to know the Bible better." These are ambiguous expressions from the lips of non-goal oriented Christians. Positive Christian living is made possible through specific goals and a daily working on them. You grow through goals. Do you have daily goals that you are working on?

PURPOSES AND GOALS

A few words need to be said about the difference between goals and purposes. A purpose is an aim or direction. It is an overall objective that we want to achieve, but as a general rule it is not fully measurable. For example, to state that you want more Bible knowledge is a purpose. To say that you will learn the books of the Bible by June 15, or the doctrine of salvation by August 15, you have stated a specific, measurable goal. Goals have specific plans and steps of action for reaching them.

God has designated many purposes for the Christian's life. These are purposes he will pursue every day of his life. They constitute the aim of his life. Some of these major purposes are as follows:

1. Christians are created to bring pleasure to God (Revelation 4:11).

2. As members of the church we must bring glory unto God (Ephesians 3:21).

3. We must seek the kingdom of God first (Matthew 6:33).

4. Children of God must strive to be holy in daily living (I Peter 1:15, 16).

5. Faithfulness is a daily aim of the Christian (Revelation 2:10).

6. We must grow in grace and knowledge (II Peter 3:18).

7. Christians must do all as unto the Lord (Ephesians 5:5-7).

8. We must grow into the fullness of Christ (Ephesians 4:11-16).

These are all major purposes in the Christian's life. In a real sense they are all tied together and relate one to another. The question is HOW are we going to accomplish these purposes?

Let's notice how goals relate to our purposes. Let's take as an example *growing in knowledge*. Note carefully the following model:

Purpose: Growth in knowledge.
(This objective may be met by setting goals such as these).
Goal One: Today I will read my Bible for 20 minutes.
Goal Two: I will take a special course in the Bible beginning September 7.
Goal Three: I will attend a special lectureship on October 15.
Goal Four: I will attend all congregational Bible classes.

Goals are always measurable. Through evidence you document your accomplishments or steps. Good goals have the ways of accomplishing, as well as deadlines. Thus, a purpose may contain many, many goals; and no ONE goal will fully accomplish the purpose that the goals relate to.

GOALS ARE BIBLICAL

It may come as a surprise to some people that the Bible exemplifies goal setting. Jesus is a good example of a person with goals. In His youth He stated one of His major purposes: "And He said unto them, How is it that ye sought me? Know ye not that I must be about my Father's business?" (Luke 1:49). In accomplishing this purpose, Jesus had some of the following goals: (1) He sought the lost (Luke 19:10); (2) He went from town to town preaching (Mark 1:38); (3) He set His mind to go to Jerusalem (Luke 9:53). The Saviour came into the world to accomplish a mission for the Father. In John 17:4 we read these words of Jesus, "I have finished the work." And on the cross, He said, ". . .it is finished" (John 19:30). Jesus accomplished His mission because He was never diverted from His goal. He didn't just blunder along hoping everything would work out in the end. His life had direction, and He worked on His goals daily. The challenge for us is to imitate our Master by establishing our purposes and goals in life.

Another example of goal setting is the apostle Paul. Note carefully his personal success formula in Philippians 3:12-14:

"Brethren, I do not regard myself as having laid hold of it yet; but one thing I do: forgetting what lies behind and reaching forward to what lies ahead. I press on toward the goal for the prize of the upward call of God in Christ Jesus."

The following brief analysis of these verses will reveal some dynamic, Biblical keys for setting and reaching goals. The verses constitute a sound success formula.

First, Paul acknowledged that achievement is a continual process, and does not come quickly: "Not that I have already obtained." It takes a person of deep conviction and humility to make such a statement. The church has an ever-challenging goal before her – to preach the gospel to every creature – that she must not shirk from or give up on because it seems too hard. Success requires work.

27

Second, Paul set goals and kept his eyes upon them. He said, ". . .this one thing I do. . ." He knew where he was going and how he was going to get there. He moved with passion and dedication toward his goals. We will never reach the goals we have set without this same dedication. Every success book agrees with Paul's statement about goals.

Third, he refused to dwell on the past; whether in the areas of success or failure, the past was behind. He said, ". . .forgetting those things which are behind. . ." A good leader realizes that dwelling on past failures could be disastrous. Likewise, past success does not ensure one today. We learn from past failures and successes, but today is a new challenge.

Fourth, Paul was excited about challenges and possibilities ahead of him. He said, ". . .reaching forth to those things which are before. . ." He was enthusiastic about the future and knew that he must be willing to cope with it. All leaders love challenges and opportunities brought by a new day, etc.

Fifth, Paul, the dynamic leader, never gave up or lost his desire. He said, ". . .I press on. . ." As a leader, he was willing to work and agonize toward reaching his "mark". It is only by personal discipline and determination that worthwhile goals are achieved.

Sixth, the apostle never doubted, with God's help, that he would acquire "the prize" sought. He had the optimism of a winner; even though he was still running the race, he knew he would win. Reward.

Seventh, as a man with many tasks and desires before him, Paul never lost sight of his priority: "of the high calling of God." With his priorities in focus and God's help he succeeded.

Before closing, I would like to note two additional passages of scripture written by Paul and add two additional qualities to his success formula (there are many others). One of the qualities is POSITIVE THINKING. In Romans 8:31, Paul wrote, "If God be for us, who can be against us?" Another quality is SELF-CONFIDENCE. To the Philippians, he wrote, "I can do all things through Christ which strengtheneth me" (Philippians 4:13). In summary, Paul's success formula consists of the following nine points:

1. Diligent work is involved in success.
2. Set goals and keep your eyes upon them.
3. Do not dwell in the past.
4. Be enthusiastic about opportunities and challenges.
5. Never give up or lose your desire.
6. Never leave God out of your plans.
7. Keep your priorities in their proper order.
8. Be a positive thinker.
9. Have confidence in yourself (Christ will help).

Whether it is on the job, in the church, in the community, at school or in the home, we, too, can succeed if we use Paul's formula for success. Take your Bible and see how many additional qualities you can deduct from Paul's life and add them to the above list.

A BASIC APPROACH TO GOAL SETTING

There are many approaches used in goal setting. Some of these are simple, and some are very complex. I want to share with you a very simple approach to goal setting. This approach has been used by many with success as they have taken it from my book *LEADERSHIP AND CHURCH GROWTH* (Lambert Bookhouse, Shreveport, LA. 1976). The following is a sample usage of this approach:

PURPOSE: To be a better husband.

OBJECTIVE: To be more considerate of my wife.

GOAL: 1. To pick up my clothes and other items I normally leave behind.

Fulfillment   a. I was careful to put my dirty
Approach: clothing into the hamper.
                  b. I put the newspaper in the garbage when I was finished with it.
                  c. I encouraged the children to do likewise.
                  d. I even picked up some of my wife's clothes.

GOAL:	2.	To show my wife more love.
Fulfillment		a. I sent her some flowers.
Approach:		b. I told her, "I love you."
		c. I took her out for dinner.
		d. I practiced being courteous.

GOAL:	3.	To purchase some time saving item.
Fulfillment		a. I saved five dollars per pay day.
Approach:		b. I cut a picture out of the paper of the item and carried it in my billfold, and looked at it daily.
		c. I bought her a dishwasher.

No matter what approach you take in goal setting, it will contain these ingredients, even though they may be stated differently. You can take this example, therefore and adapt it to EVERY area of your personal and business life, as well as your spiritual life. It will work if you will work!

BASIC GUIDELINES FOR SETTING GOALS

Goal setting is a challenging process. Thus we need some workable guidelines to help us in this important area of being a winner. In setting and working toward goals, the following things should be remembered.

FIRST, WORK ON ONE GOAL ÀT A TIME. Be specific when you set a goal. Be sure that it is the most meaningful goal for you at this time in your life. Crystallize your thinking and move ahead with singleness of purpose. Keep your eyes on the target. I've made the mistake of trying to work on too many goals at one time. It can lead to defeat. Therefore, set and work on one goal at a time in each area of your life. This is a must!

SECOND, WRITE DOWN YOUR GOAL. State it in clear, honest, understandable terms. Do not fool yourself or try to be too spiritual. Seeing your goal on paper will give you visual motivation. Each day as you take it out of your pocket or purse, you will be reminded of where you are going. Thus carry it on your person at all times.

THIRD, THINK ABOUT YOUR GOAL FREQUENTLY (DAILY). This will occur when you take the paper you have written your goal on and look at it during the course of the day. Think about your goal. Form a mental picture of your goal and see yourself reaching it.

FOURTH, SET A DEADLINE FOR REACHING YOUR GOAL. Do not use the nebulous "someday" approach. "Someday" will never come. Set the month and year you plan for your goal to be reached. Some men, for example in the space program, go so far as to set the day, month and hour they will reach their goal.

FIFTH, DON'T BECOME DISCOURAGED. It is very human to become discouraged. The key, as we have pointed out time and time again, is not to let discouragement be turned into defeat. Don't Stop! You are a winner, in the process of winning. Keep a burning desire to achieve your goal. Be confident, God will help. Nothing can defeat determination. Try ONE more time!

SIXTH, BE WILLING TO MAKE CHANGES. No one, in the final analysis, really knows what shall be on the next day (cf. James 4:14-18). Therefore, many unexpected things may come up as you move toward your goal. You must be flexible and change if necessary. Be sure, however, that changes do not alter your goal (if the goal is still possible). Remember this: it is permissible to take a rest stop on the way to your goal, as you work on making the changes needed to reach your goal. Change if needed.

SEVENTH, WORK DILIGENTLY EACH DAY ON YOUR GOAL. This factor has been stressed throughout this book; I hope by now the point is clear in your mind. The only place success is found before work is in the dictionary. Approach your work with enthusiasm. Remember, your goal is worth it. Always be a DOER!

EIGHTH, REMEMBER IT IS EXCITING AND YOUTHFUL TO ALWAYS HAVE SOMETHING TO LOOK FORWARD TO. A person without a plan and goal in life is not long for life. Emerson rightly said, "We do not count a

31

man's years, until he has nothing else to count." A person with a goal will always have something to count.

NINTH, BE SURE YOU HAVE ALL THE ESSENTIAL FACTS. This is why goal setting and planning involves time. You will need all the facts before you launch out toward your goal. Do your homework. Get all the facts and then use them to your advantage in reaching your goal.

TENTH, REMEMBER THE VARIOUS LEVELS OF PLANNING AND GOAL SETTING. Goals are of a great variety, and exist on all levels. Some of these levels are: (a) your TOTAL life goals; (b) your 5-10-15 year plan; (c) your plans for a year; (d) your plans for six months; (e) your plans for a month; (f) your plans for a week; (g) your plans for a day; and (h) your plans for several hours. This is known as long and short range planning. Both areas are musts if you plan to be a continual winner.

ELEVENTH, BE SURE TO PROPERLY APPROACH YOUR DAILY PLANS. As already stressed in this book, if success occurs, it will do so - TODAY!. Therefore, you must make your plans for today. The following suggestions will help you prepare a goal list for each day:

1. Write tomorrow's goals down tonight.
2. Goals become a "Things To Do" list.
3. Pray over your goals, asking God for help.
4. List your goals according to their importance.
5. Look at your list in the morning before you depart for work, etc.
6. Start, without delay, on your number one item.
7. Review your goals at lunch (you may also look at your list of long range goals, etc.).
8. Make any adjustments needed in daily goals.
9. Review your list when the day is over and evaluate your progress. Be sure to note any weaknesses and why. How will you do better tomorrow?
10. Prepare tomorrow's list, etc.
11. Remember you are a winner, daily.
12. DON'T STOP! SUCCESS IS JUST AHEAD.

BASIC STRATEGY FOR GOAL SETTING

Here is a master planning guide to use in setting your goals. It's just another approach to goal setting. To gain maximum benefits from it, I suggest that you copy it on a separate sheet of paper and use it daily.

Fill in each area below very thoroughly:

1. Here, in specific words is what I plan to accomplish.

2. This is HOW I will accomplish the above stated goal.

3. This is the date the above goal will be achieved.

4. Here are some of the possible challenges - problems - obstacles - I might meet in reaching the above goal:

     a.
     b.
     c.
     d.
     e.

5. Here are the steps I will take to overcome each challenge - problem - obstacle:

     a.
     b.
     c.
     d.
     e.

6. I must remember, and use if possible, the following sources or helps in reaching my objective:

     a.
     b.
     c.
     d.

7. In reaching my goal I will:

    a. Use my creative imagination every day. I will think of new and better ways to do things, etc.
    b. Make specific plans of action to reach my goal.
    c. I will "see" each step I must take to reach my goal.
    d. Live with my daily goals before me in a written form.
    e. Let nothing stand in my way, but the Lord's will.
    f. Live like a winner, because I am winning.
    g. Carry my goals in my pocket or purse, written on paper so I can see them when I want to.
    h. Pray about my goals daily.
    i. Work–work–work–work–toward my goals.
    j. I won't STOP.

There you have it - a basic, common sense approach to setting and reaching goals. I guarantee you that it will work if you will put it into action on a daily basis.

FOR THOUGHT AND DISCUSSION

1. Do you have a set of goals?
2. What is the difference between a purpose and a goal?
3. Discuss the major purposes of the Christian life.
4. Write out a set of goals for growing in Bible knowledge.
5. Why do some persons think goals aren't Biblical?
6. Discuss Paul's success formula.
7. Can you think of other passages in the Bible that relate to success?
8. What would you tell a person who doesn't have a set of goals?

9. What are the biggest hindrances to goal setting and reaching them?

10. How do you plan to use this lesson?

CHAPTER FIVE

BALANCING LIFE'S WHEEL

How balanced is your life? Have you given much thought to this question? Take a few minutes and think about it.

    * A car with wheels out of balance produces a rough ride.

    * A balance of trade is essential for a strong economy.

    * A balance of power is important to world peace.

    * Accuracy of a watch depends on a balance wheel.

    * An unbalanced diet contributes to poor health.

    * A failure to properly balance your check book may lead to financial trouble.

    * A balance in nature insures us of a safe environment.

    * A balanced exercise program leads to better physical fitness.

From these eight illustrations we are reminded that balance is important in every area of life. But it is to *life* itself that balance has the greatest application. A life out of balance can't live a positive Christian life. An unbalanced life will never have the peace and happiness promised by Jesus when He said, "I have come that you may have life, and have it more abundantly" (John 10:10). This abundancy is not limited, as some seem to think, to a few areas of life. It is a promise of TOTAL life to the man who will follow Jesus as Lord.

What do you think of when you think of a person who is living a life that is out of balance?

How would you define balance? A teenager defined it in these words, "It is getting it all together." Another person defined it this way, "It is placing equal emphasis upon all areas of your life."

Webster gives many definitions of balance; some of them are: "equilibrium, stability, harmonious proportion, equal." The positive Christian is interested in harmonious proportion for his life. This is essential to positive, successful Christian living.

Most persons are in agreement that there are six major areas of life that must be balanced. These six areas constitute life's wheel. Imagine a wheel with six spokes in it; each representing an area of your life. Thus, if things are to run smoothly in your life, you must balance each of the following areas by giving them proper emphasis. An over-emphasis on one, to the neglecting of others, will lead to an unbalanced life.

First, there is the spiritual area. This has to do with man's religion. What are your goals in the spiritual area of your life? Paul tells us that it is "unto a perfect man, unto the measure of the stature of the fullness of Christ" (cf. Ephesians 4:11-16). Thus your goal is to be more like Jesus today than you were yesterday. To develop in this area, which is really the center of your life, you must strive to have the mind of Christ (cf. Philippians 2:5-8). This means that you try to think like Jesus would think in every situation. This is why you must renew the inward man day by day (cf. II Corinthians 4:16). In II Peter 1:5-7 the apostle Peter gives us a list of qualities that we must add to our lives in order to develop the spiritual man.

There are some persons who believe that a man must give his total time to prayer, fasting, good deeds, etc. To do this they suggest that a monastery would be a good place to go. On the other hand there are those who would neglect the inward man altogether. God desires a balance. A balance that comes only through His word being stored in the heart (cf. James 1:19-22). This is the area most essential for balance in your TOTAL life.

Second, the family must be given proper time and attention. The Bible admonishes husbands to love their wives, and wives to love their husbands (cf. Ephesians 5:22-23). Likewise, children are told to obey their parents (cf. Ephesians 6:2-4). The father is the head of the house and, therefore, responsible for carrying out God's plan for balance in the home (cf. Proverbs 22:6; 23:13-15).

The homes of our day are more neglected than ever before. This is evidenced by the divorce rate and other problems. The child of God must not neglect his family. He must plan his time so as to have some for his family. He must not ignore or abuse them. How balanced is your family life?

Third, the social area of your life is important. Many Christians act as though they have been called out of the world as well as out of relationship with humanity, as they seclude themselves from their brethren.

Jesus provides us with a good example of being sociable. Luke says of Him, "And Jesus increased in wisdom and stature, and in favour with God and man" (Luke 2:52). It is interesting to note how many social functions Jesus attended (e.g., wedding, meals, etc.). Surely if the Son of God thought they were important, we must think so, too. This is why every Christian is admonished to be given to hospitality (cf. Romans 12:13). How sociable are you? Do you take time to be with people? This is part of a balanced life.

Fourth, the vocational or job area of life must be properly handled. Many Christians have failed to understand God's emphasis upon working. Paul said that if a man won't work, don't let him eat (cf. II Thessalonians 3:10). This is strong language, but it lets us know how God feels about laziness. The Christian gives a day of work for a day's pay.

We are told that if a Christian will perform his work as unto the Lord, he will be blessed for it (cf. Ephesians 6:5-9). If practiced, this would guarantee a new attitude toward work. It would also help the man on the job to know that his labor is not *secular* because he is doing it for the Lord. This helps us to remember that Christianity is not a *way of life,* it is TOTAL LIFE. A life that is lived 24 hours per day for the Lord.

Fifth, Christians must realize the need for proper recreation in their lives. Some seem to think that this is out of harmony with Christianity. Not so! The apostle John wrote, "Beloved, I wish above all things that thou mayest prosper and be in health, even as thy soul prospereth" (III John 2). God desires balance in your life.

Christians must take good care of themselves physically. Jesus recognized the need for rest and said, ". . .come ye yourselves apart into a desert place, and rest a while: for there were many coming and going, and they had no leisure so much as to eat" (Mark 6:31).

God's children must not allow themselves to become overweight or indulgent in any habits that would ruin their good health or example of being Christ-like. You must remember that your body is the temple of the Holy Spirit (cf. I Corinthians 6:19). This should encourage you to take proper care of it. Paul said, "For bodily exercise profiteth little. . ." (I Timothy 4:8). In the Greek the meaning is that bodily exercise profits for a *little time.* Thus, exercise does have some profit. To balance your life you must not neglect the recreational area.

Sixth, the financial aspect of your life must be properly balanced. For many Christians this is the area that throws the total wheel of life out of balance. They find it hard to manage their finances. It is the source of many problems in the family and in the church. Paul said, "Moreover it is required in stewards, that a man be found faithful" (I Corinthians 4:2).

Jesus gives us some sound advice for investment: "Lay not up for yourselves treasures upon earth. . .But lay up for yourselves treasures in heaven. . .For where your treasure is, there will your heart be also" (Matthew 6:19-21). It is not wrong for you to have money. In fact, God gives you the power to get wealth (cf. Deuteronomy 8:18). The challenge, however, is to properly manage that which comes into your hands.

These six areas provide us with daily challenges to balance our lives. To the degree that we have them all in focus and under control, to that degree we have a balanced life. An overemphasis on any one area, to the neglecting of others, will produce an unbalanced life.

How balanced is your life? To help you answer this question please work the following personal evaluation section.

1. My greatest spiritual strength is _____

_____

I plan to make the following spiritual improvements _____

_____

2. My greatest family strength is _____

I plan to make the following improvements in my family life _____

_____

3. My greatest social strength is_____

I plan to make the following improvements in the social area of my life _____

_____

4. My greatest vocational strength is _____

I plan to make the following improvements in the vocational area of my life _____

_____

5. My greatest recreational strength is_____

I plan to make the following improvements in my recreational life _____

_____

6. My greatest financial strength is _____

I plan to make the following financial improvements in my life _____

_____

FOR THOUGHT AND DISCUSSION

1. Do you agree to the six major areas of life? Can you think of others?

2. Did you complete the six areas above?

3. Why is it so hard to balance life?

4. Who is the most balanced person you know?

5. Which area of the six is the hardest to balance? Why?

6. Share some additional verses from the Bible that relate to balance.

7. What would you tell a person who said it was wrong to take a vacation?

8. Draw a wheel with six spokes and indicate with a dot on the spoke where you are as far as growth is concerned. Then draw a line from dot to dot. This will show you how balanced your life's wheel is.

9. Why do some people *worship* work?

10. How do you plan to use this lesson in your life?

CHAPTER SIX

POWER FOR MASTERING LIFE

CONSIDER THESE FACTS:
* Man has mastered the atom.
* Man has been able to transplant hearts.
* Man has been able to synthesize a gene.
* Man has been able to alter the weather.
* Man has mastered travel and distance.
* Man has mastered the art of instant data through computers.
* Man has tamed wild animals.
* Man has harnessed the energy of the sun.
* Man has brought the world together via TV.

Yet, for the most part, man has not been able to master his own personal life. It seems that he can master about everything but himself. This is the most difficult area of all. It is not a come lately challenge like some of the above mentioned things. The challenge to self-mastery has been with man since the very beginning of his existence. Since Eve failed to master her life when she was confronted by the devil, man has been on a downhill course.

HOW SOME TRY TO MASTER LIFE

Man's attempts to master life have been varied and unusual. In fact, as a general rule of thumb, it is difficult to convince a person that he, by himself, can't master his life. He thinks he can. This is why he is on a constant treadmill trying to keep up with himself and all the others around him. Some of the ways man has tried to get the upper hand on life are through some of the following things.

1. Some think strong drink will give them the courage they need to win the battles of life. This has produced more than 9 million alcoholics in our nation. "The bottle controls me," is how one alcoholic expressed his plight with the "devil's brew."

2. Drug abuse is another route taken by persons as they attempt to control their lives. They need a pill to get high, a pill to calm down, a pill to sleep, a pill to stay

42

awake, etc. Millions in our country are being mastered by the pill.

3. Some think life will be more controllable if they change jobs; thus, the rush is on. Soon, however, the new wears off and the same problems and frustrations appear. This is because the problem is within the heart of man.

4. Divorce and remarriage has been viewed by many as the golden key that will set them free and give them a new control over their lives. Last year there was over 1 million divorces in the USA. Things are growing worse instead of better.

5. Moving, changing schools, and a host of other pseudo social changes have been viewed as the route to mastery over life. This too has proven to be a dead end street.

6. Meditation, time management courses, self-help seminars, and a host of other human efforts have proven fruitless as men have sought to master their lives through these avenues.

7. Self-punishment or pseudo asceticism is another approach by man in his quest for self-mastery. Through mental rigors and other self-denial approaches they think they can do it themselves.

8. Trying to get away from it all is another approach to self-mastery. This attitude sometimes sees others as being responsible for their problems in life. Becoming a "Wilderness Family" doesn't free man of himself.

These are only eight of the many ways that men in our day are trying to master their lives. There are many others. Can you think of some additional ones?

RESULTS OF NOT MASTERING LIFE

When I was in the Navy, I was stationed aboard an aircraft carrier. One of my jobs was working in the landing and launching tower. One day as the jets were in the landing pattern, a pilot radioed that he was loosing power and was going to have to set it down in the "drink."

It was a helpless feeling to stand and watch the once powerful jet slowly going down as it was loosing power.

Finally it made a "belly landing" on the sea several hundred yards from the ship. The pilot escaped without injury.

Many plane accidents have occurred because of a loss of power. Without sufficient power the pilot doesn't have control of the plane.

The need for power is not limited to planes, cars, boats, etc. Man also needs power to properly control his everyday life. Without the proper power he is on a disaster course. A crash is just ahead for the person who doesn't have power to master his life.

Everywhere you look there are crash sights. These are the results of lives not being properly mastered. Some of the more obvious signs are as follows:

1. Suicide is a major cause of death among college age persons in our country. "Life is a bum trip" is how one teenager expressed it in his suicide note. Not long ago I read of a millionaire who committed suicide. This is the end result, in most cases, of an unmastered life.

2. Unhappiness is another common symptom of an unmastered life. Ulcers, heartburn, and a host of other aches and pains are produced through unhappy minds. The local bar reminds us that the "Happy Hour" is only between 5 and 6. How about the rest of the day?

3. No zest for living. They can't stand the here and now. They don't want to go back to yesterday; and they are afraid of the future.

4. Misery and guilt are the products of an uncontrolled life. There is no rest for the person weary in sin.

5. A life of sin and rebellion against God (cf. James 1:13-17). Deeper and deeper into sin a person goes without God.

6. Conflict and problems with other people.

7. The best summary of an uncontrolled life is found in Romans 1:24-32:

> "Therefore God gave them over in the sinful desires of their hearts to sexual impurity for the degrading of their bodies with one another. . .In the same way the men also abandoned natural relations with women and were inflamed with lust

for one another. . .They have become filled with every kind of wickedness, evil, greed and depravity. They are full of envy, murder, strife, deceit and malice. They are gossips, slanderers, God-haters, insolent, arrogant and boastful; they are senseless, faithless, heartless, ruthless." (NIV).

POWER FOR MASTERING LIFE

A few evenings ago my 9 year-old son became frustrated as he was trying to lift his barbells. Try as he may, he didn't have the power to lift the additional weight he had placed on the bar. All of his struggling was in vain. He didn't have the power.

Man through his own power, try as he may, can't handle the burdens and pressures of life. He needs a power stronger than himself. He needs a power outside of himself. There is such a power.

To a world wrecked by sin, Jesus announced, "I have come that they may have life, and have it to the full" (John 10:10). The apostle Peter wrote, "His divine power has given us everything we need for life and godliness through our knowledge of Him who called us. . ." (II Peter 1:3).

Since God grants us real life through His Son, it must also be true that He gives us power to maintain this life. This is true because He desires that we remain faithful until death (cf. Revelation 2:10).

The power doesn't come easy after conversion to Christ. The apostle Paul said, "For the good that I would I do not: but the evil which I would not, that I do. . .I find then a law, that, when I would do good, evil is present with me. . .O wretched man that I am! who shall deliver me from the body of this death? I thank God through Christ our Lord. . ." (Romans 7:20-25). A person, therefore, must work on developing self-control (cf. II Peter 1:5-7). To get control over life and self, I believe some of the following things are essential to controlling one's life.

First, a person must want to master his life. This is the base of all positive actions. As Paul, we must "serve the

45

law of God with our minds" (cf. Romans 7:25).

Second, your life must be right with God. He gives power to win over self (cf. I John 4:4). Sin will cripple one's ability to master his life.

Third, unreserved faith must be held in Christ. He is the way, the truth and the life (cf. John 14:6). We must believe that He is able to keep that which we have committed to His trust.

Fourth, you must believe that Christ is "able to do exceedingly abundantly above all that we ask or think, according to the power that worketh in us" (Ephesians 3:20).

Fifth, there must be a daily renewal of your mind (cf. Ephesians 23). This is the results of a definite resolution: e.g., "I now renew my mind" (May be uttered in prayer).

Sixth, your thinking must be directed by the word of God (cf. Psalm 119:97ff; James 1:18-24). It must become the basis of ALL decisions.

Seventh, you must pray for wisdom on a daily basis. God has promised to give us wisdom if we will ask for it (cf. James 1:5).

Eighth, a person must daily deny himself (cf. Matthew 16:24). This evidences his trust in Christ as the Master of his life.

Ninth, you must be led by the Spirit. Paul said, "For as many as are led by the Spirit of God, they are the sons of God" (Romans 8:14).

Tenth, to master your life you must believe that you can do ALL things through Christ (cf. Philippians 4:13). "But my God shall supply all your needs according to his riches in glory by Christ Jesus" (Philippians 4:19).

Eleventh, to master life you must have a positive spiritual attitude. This requires proper input into the mind.

Medical technology is a wonderful thing. Not long ago I saw a lady on TV who was "being kept alive" by a life support system. "If it is unplugged," her husband said, "she will die."

Christ is more than our life *support*. Paul said: "For ye are dead, and your life is hid with Christ in God. When Christ, WHO IS OUR LIFE, shall appear, then shall we also appear with him in glory" (Colossians 3:3, 4). Christ is OUR LIFE! And as long as we stay in Him (cf. Ephesians 1:3;

I John 1:7), we have power—His power—to master life. Have you yielded to Him today?

FOR THOUGHT AND DISCUSSION

1. Why is it important to have control of your life?

2. Why is self-discipline such a great problem in our country?

3. Can you think of additional wrong ways persons try to master life?

4. Discuss some additional results of not mastering life.

5. Discuss the points relating to power for mastering life.

6. How would you help a person who eats too much?

7. What are some extreme examples of self-mastery?

8. Do you have a personal plan for mastering the problem areas of your life?

9. Share some additional verses from the Bible on mastering life.

10. How do you plan to use this lesson in your life?

CHAPTER SEVEN

BIBLICAL-CYBERNETICS:
A SAFE GUIDANCE SYSTEM

"Men give advice; God gives guidance."

"What if the guidance system fails?" is a frequent question asked by persons who are concerned about various missile launching sights around the world.

If you are like most people you are probably fascinated by the potentials of guided missiles. It's amazing what these weapons have become since the first building and testing of them in the USA during 1916 to 1918. The first guided missiles had pre-set controls, which means that their first target could not be changed in flight. From this simple beginning missile guidance has developed into four main guidance systems, or by a combination of these four: (1) Beam Rider, (2) Pre-set, (3) Command, and (4) Homing.

In a sense man is like a missile: he is headed to a destiny. He was launched on this destiny at birth. To properly reach his target, in the spiritual sense, heaven, he must have a proper, fail-proof guidance system. In a word he needs a "command" guidance system.

In a real missile command guidance system, a human pilot on the ground sends commands to the missile to steer it in flight. In spiritual command guidance, the person must send commands to his heart (mind) in order to stay on the beam and reach his ultimate target of heaven.

Not only does a person need a proper guidance system for reaching heaven, he also needs one for reaching the daily success targets in life. I have some wonderful news for you. There is ONE guidance system that can guide you to EVERY target (goal), both spiritual and physical, that you want to reach. This guidance system is biblical-cybernetics. It is a guidance system given by God that never fails if you properly use it.

BIBLICAL-CYBERNETICS

In defining cybernetics, Dr. Maxwell Maltz, states, "The word 'cybernetics' comes from the Greek word which means literally, 'the steerman.' " (p. 17, Psycho-Cyber-netics).

Webster defines cybernetic (Gr. kybernetes, helms-man; + ics), a word coined in 1948 by Norbert Wiener, as "a science dealing with the comparative study of complex electronic calculating machines and the human nervous system in an attempt to explain the nature of the brain."

The Greek word *kybernan,* which is usually trans-lated *govern,* means "to exercise control over; control."

Biblical-cybernetics therefore is the usage of God's word (i.e., the Holy Bible) as the "steersman for our lives." It sets forth the Bible as the *only* safe guidance system for man. The wise man of old stated it this way: "Thy word is a lamp unto my feet, and a light unto my path. . .The en-trance of thy words giveth light; it giveth understanding unto the simple. . .Order my steps in thy word. . ." (Psalm 119:105, 130, 133). Herbert Hoover said this: "There is no other book so various as the Bible, nor so full of con-centrated wisdom. Whether it be of law, business, morals or that vision which leads the imagination in the creation of constructive enterprises. . .he who seeks for guidance. . . may look inside its covers and find illumination."

Biblical-cybernetics is the answer to man's need and desire for proper piloting through the seas of life. This steersman can get you to your destiny when all others have failed. It is sad that some persons wait until it is almost too late before they start using biblical-cybernetics to guide them to success and happiness. A person is wise who starts young in letting the Bible be his guide. The prophet Jeremiah said: "O Lord, I know that the way of man is not in himself: it is not in man that walketh to direct his steps" (Jeremiah 10:23). This is why we need a safe guidance system like biblical-cybernetics. Positive Christian living is possible through daily application of God's word.

In summary biblical-cybernetics consist of the fol-lowing facts:

1. *Directional* thinking through biblical principles. The Bible tells us how, what, when, and where to do (and act).

2. Proven *methods* based upon a balanced view of

man. This system is concerned with the whole man: body, soul and spirit.

3. The *fundamentals* of all other sound, honorable success principles. This is back to basics.

4. A *non-threatening* approach to success and happiness. God knows what will work for His creation. God's word doesn't go out of style.

5. Principles *approved* by the Creator. This is not true of all the success principles developed by man.

6. Biblical-cybernetics is *relevant* to every situation. ("What does the Bible say?")

7. *Practical* and *usable* principles for reaching EVERY goal in your life.

8. *Other person* centered. Not an ego or selfish approach to life.

9. *Encouraging* approach to success and happiness. It gives you hope: you can make it.

10. *Acceptable* approach to achieving the good life. All will agree to the soundness of biblical-cybernetics.

If you desire success and happiness, it will come through guidance from God's word (the Bible). It is the word of God that must give direction to the brain of man. Listen again to the wise man as he relates the power of God's word for good: "Thy word have I hid in my heart, that I might not sin against thee" (Psalm 119:11); "Thy testimonies also are my delight and my counselors" (Psalm 119:24). It was Jesus who said, ". . .It is written, man shall not live by bread alone, but by every word that proceedeth out of the mouth of God" (Matthew 4:4). Thus the word of God is a powerful tool for our every need. Through guidance from it we can reach every goal.

In the chapters of this book there are many success and happiness principles. All of them are based upon the Bible. They constitute the basic system of biblical-cybernetics. If you will let them guide you, you will achieve these great objectives: success and happiness. Let biblical-cybernetics be your steersman on a daily basis and you will reach your goals. Start today! Do it NOW! Positive Christianity depends upon it.

A minister was once asked without prior notice to conduct a service in a home. He called for a Bible, but none was found. At last, however, they found one in an old sea chest in the attic. Strange to say, on the outside were the words, "Not wanted on the voyage." I hope this is not your case. Be sure you make the voyage through life with God's word as your steersman. Let biblical-cybernetics show you the way, as you learn His word. Happy steering!

WHY STUDY THE BIBLE?

Why study the Bible? This is a very good question, and one that is asked very often. Some have the mistaken idea that since they have obeyed the gospel, there is no need to do any more studying in the Bible. "After all," they say, "I have done the important part." The important part does not end here.

We should study the Bible not just to win arguments or display our great knowledge of the Bible, as some do. But, rather, we should study the Bible for the great spiritual benefits that are to be derived from such studies. We should study the Bible because it is interesting, unique, and without equal in the literary field. But above all, we should study the Bible because of the value it has upon the souls of men; more especially, the value it has on MY soul. A few reasons for studying the Bible are as follows:

1. We must study God's Word because a lack of knowledge leads to destruction (Hosea 4:6).

2. We must study God's Word because an error will condemn (II Thessalonians 1:7-9).

3. We must study God's Word because it will make us wise unto salvation (II Timothy 3:15).

4. We must study God's Word because we are commanded to do so (II Timothy 2:15).

5. We must study God's Word because it is the "seed" of the kingdom (Luke 8:11).

6. We must study God's Word because it will assist us in spiritual growth (I Peter 2:1, 2).

7. We must study God's Word because it helps us keep our souls saved (James 1:21).

8. We must study God's Word because it helps supply virtues to our faith (II Peter 1:5-8).

9. We must study the Bible because it was written for our learning (Romans 15:4).

10. We must study the Bible because it helps us "be doers of the word" (James 1:22).

11. We must study the Bible because man is not able to direct his steps; therefore, the word provides guidance (Psalm 119:105, Jeremiah 10:23; Matthew 15:14).

12. We must study the Bible because it contains God's will for time and eternity (His will for my life) (I Corinthians 15:51-54; I Peter 1:2-5; Hebrews 5:8, 9).

13. We must study the Bible so that we may be able to teach others (Matthew 28:19, 20; II Timothy 2:2).

14. We must study the Bible because it provides comfort (Romans 15:4).

15. We must study the Bible because it is true (John 8:32; 17:17; Acts 17:11).

16. We must study the Bible because in it, we learn about God and His attributes (John 17:3).

17. We must study the Bible because Christ set the example (Luke 24:27; 24:32).

18. We must study the Bible because it is our spiritual diet (Hebrews 5:12-14).

19. We must study the Bible because it will keep us from falling (Hebrews 6:1-6).

20. Read Psalm 119 to see many other things that the Word is able to do. These serve as additional reasons for studying God's Word.

"Study the Bible to be wise; believe it to be safe; practice it to be holy." --Unknown

FOR THOUGHT AND DISCUSSION

1. How is man like a missile?
2. What is man's target in life? After death?
3. What is cybernetics?
4. What is directional thinking?
5. What is redirectional thinking?
6. Why is the Bible a safe guide?
7. What would you tell a person who doesn't think Bible study is important?
8. Discuss James 1:19-23.

9. How has thinking on the word of God helped you?

10. How do you plan to use this lesson in your daily life?

CHAPTER EIGHT

YOUR MIND: THE SEAT OF POSITIVE
CHRISTIAN LIVING

Nothing has fascinated man more than the human mind. Every generation has sought to discover its full potentials. It has been called "the great frontier." A prominent psychologist, William James, said that one of the greatest discoveries of our age is the fact that men can change their lives by changing their thinking.

If scientists were able to build an electronic computer that matched the nerve connection of the human brain, they would need a skyscraper to house it, the power of Niagara Falls to run it, and the water of Niagara to cool it. Yet God has compressed it all into the small space of a cranium. The brain of man can record 800 memories each second. This can continue for the space of 70 to 80 years without getting tired. No man-made computer, no matter how advanced, can match the ability and service of the human brain. David was certainly right when he said, "I will praise thee; for I am fearfully and wonderfully made: marvelous are thy works; and that my soul knoweth right well" (Psalm 139:14).

The mind of man is neglected. It has been said over and over that man only uses about 7 to 10 percent of his brain during his lifetime. Even the percent that man uses is manipulated in one way or another. In discussing the crippling effect TV has on students, Jeffery Schrank, in his book *Snap, Crackle and Popular Taste,* says, "Producers of filmstrips for high-school students now find that they leave a single picture on the screen only for an average of eight seconds or else students become bored." (pp. 26, 27). Their attention span, which is a product of mind control, has been ruined by too much TV watching.

Vance Packard, in his book *The Hidden Persuaders,* wrote, ". . .seven out of ten of today's purchases are decided in the store, where the shoppers buy on impulse!!!" Packard reports that other studies reveal that as much as 90 percent of purchases are made through impulse buying. All of this is saying that man doesn't use his mind in making daily decisions. He lets others control his mind.

Another indictment against man and his mind is the charge that man doesn't concentrate on one subject, item or thought for as much as ten seconds per day. George Bernard Shaw was bold enough to say, "Few people think more than two or three times a year; I have made an international reputation for myself by thinking once or twice a week."

Christians are not exempt from the charges against neglecting usage of the mind. Many have failed to look after, and use properly, the mind that God has given them. No thinking, improper thinking, fatigue, too much study, living on drugs, and many other things have had a serious effect upon the thinking of Christians. "The diseases of the mind," said Cicero, "are more destructive than those of the body."

The victorious Christian life depends upon how you use your mind. Positive Christian living begins in the mind. Until your mind is brought under control you will fall short of God's goals for your life. Paul said, "For to be carnally minded is death; but to be spiritually minded is life and peace" (Romans 8:6). This is why Christians must nurture their minds with proper thoughts; they must have control of their minds at all times.

TROUBLE IN MIND

When God created man he was perfect and upright. It wasn't long, however, before his thoughts became set on evil: "And God saw that the wickedness of man was great in the earth, and that every imagination of the thoughts of his heart was only evil continually" (Genesis 6:5). ". . .for the imagination of man's heart is evil from his youth. . ." (Genesis 8:21). Man is in his present state of trouble because of the thoughts which have ruled his life. Jeremiah said evil imagination is one of the reasons why Israel fell (cf. Jeremiah 3:17; 9:14, 13:10). It is still destroying people.

I am told that computer programmers pay special attention to what they feed into a computer. They know they will get out ONLY what they put in. G-I-G-O is a computer acronym, and not the name of a pizza parlor. G-I-G-O stands for Good In, Good Out; or Garbage In, Garbage Out.

Thus if garbage goes in, garbage will come out.

G-I-G-O has an application to the mind of man. If you put garbage (wrong thinking) in, you will get garbage out (wrong living). This is in harmony with the law of sowing and reaping. The apostle Paul wrote: "Be not deceived; God is not mocked: for whatsoever a man soweth, that shall he also reap. For he that soweth to his flesh shall of the flesh reap corruption; but he that soweth to the Spirit shall of the Spirit reap life everlasting" (Galatians 6:7, 8). You are what you think (cf. Proverbs 23:7). You will harvest the crop from the seed you have sown.

The mind of man has become the sowing ground for all kinds of corrupt seed. It has become a place to dump garbage of every description. Pornography has become a multi-million dollar business because people are filling their minds with this garbage. TV is another popular way to fill the mind with garbage. By the time a person reaches 18 years of age in American society it is estimated that he has watched 25,000 hours of TV; 350,000 commercials consume some of this time. There is no way of knowing how many homes have broken up by soap operas, as the characters on these programs have influenced the American housewife. (Many husbands also watch). Every crime in the book has been attributed by some to the influence of TV in the lives of criminals. After NBC showed the film *The Doomsday Flight* in 1966, bomb threats increased 300 percent over the previous month. The power of suggestion to an uncontrolled mind is without limits or bounds. Jesus put it this way: "A good man out of the good treasure of the heart bringeth forth evil things" (Matthew 12:35). One of the seven abominations that God hates is a heart that deviseth wicked imaginations (cf. Proverbs 6:16-18).

The chambers of man's mind is the developing ground for every wicked deed. In many cases, in fact probably in most cases, it is not possible to really know what is going on inside of man's mind. If we had lived in the days of Ezekiel we would have seen "holy men" working in the sanctuary of God. By all outward appearances they were doing their duty to God. But when we, along with Ezekiel, look into the chambers of their minds, we find the opposite is true. In their minds they were serving Tammuz the heathen sun god (cf. Ezekiel 8:1-18). True service is in the heart.

What are you in the chambers of your mind? This is one of the most important questions you will ever answer. The answer will reveal the REAL you. What are your hidden thoughts? What kind of "movies" do you show in the chambers of your mind? To the degree they are evil or wicked, to that degree your life is out of harmony with God's will for your life. To live a positive Christian life you must clean up the chambers of your mind. If you don't the end results is described by Paul in Romans, chapter one. He said, "But that, when they knew God, they glorified him not as God, neither were thankful; but became vain in their imaginations and their foolish heart was darkened. . .Wherefore God also gave them up. . ." (Romans 1:21, 24). You will reap what you sow!

GOD'S PROGRAM FOR YOUR MIND

Jesus made it clear that man's problem is not what comes into his stomach. Eating is not what defiles him (cf. Mark 7:14-19). Christ said, ". . .That which cometh out of man, that defileth the man. For from within, out of the heart of men, proceed *evil thoughts*, adulteries, fornication, murders, thefts, covetousness, wickedness, deceit, lasciviousness, an evil eye, blasphemy, pride, foolishness: All these evil things come from WITHIN, and defile the man" (Mark 7:20-23). Man's thinking is what defiles him. This is why repentance, which means to *change the mind,* is essential to salvation (cf. Luke 13:3, Acts 17:30, 31).

After a person "changes his mind," he must continue to maintain that changed mind. To do this, the Christian must program his mind daily with God's word. Isaiah said, "Thou wilt keep him in perfect peace, whose MIND is stayed on Thee: because he trusteth in Thee" (Isaiah 26:3). The key to proper programming of your mind is found in the words of the Psalmist, "O how love I thy law! it is my meditation ALL THE DAY" (Psalm 119:97). Some of the specific things that you must do for your mind are seen in the following verses. This is a biblical G-I-G-O: God's plan for putting good into your mind. Take your Bible and look up each reference and study it very carefully, because "out of the heart are the issues of life" (Proverbs 19:14).

1. Each Christian must seek to have the mind of Christ (Philippians 2:5).

2. You must gird up the loins of your mind (I Peter 3:1).

3. Let God's word stir up your mind (II Peter 3:1).

4. Christians should arm themselves with the same mind (I Peter 4:1).

5. Proper living is based upon renewing your mind (Romans 12:2).

6. You have a goal of keeping your mind (Philippians 4:7).

7. Don't be shaken in your mind (II Thessalonians 2:2).

8. Christians must be sober minded (Titus 2:6).

9. We must serve the Lord with our mind (Romans 7:25).

10. Successful work depends upon the mind (Nehemiah 4:6).

11. We must daily renew our minds (Ephesians 4:23).

12. Don't become wearied in mind (Hebrews 12:3).

13. We must mind the same rule (Philippians 3:6).

14. A carnal mind makes you an enemy of God (Romans 8:7).

15. We must think high thoughts (Isaiah 55:8).

16. Love thinketh no evil (I Corinthians 13:5).

17. We must forsake wicked thoughts (Isaiah 55:7).

18. You must set your mind on things that are above (Colossians 3:2).

19. Persuasion occurs in the mind (Romans 14:5).

20. Place the word in your heart (Psalm119:11).

21. Perform God's statutes from the heart (Psalm 119:112).

22. Think on these things (Philippians 4:7-9).

23. A double minded man is unstable (James 1:8).

24. The word helps you exercise your senses (Hebrews 5:13, 14).

25. God's word must be in our minds (Hebrews 8:10; 10:16).

Your mind is the seat of positive Christian living. To grow into the fullness of Christ you must fill your mind with good, wholesome, truthful thoughts. Pliny said, "As land is improved by sowing it with various seeds, so is the mind by exercising it with different studies." "Cultivation of the mind," said Cicero, "is as necessary as food to the body." In Isaiah, God makes a promise: "Thou wilt keep him in perfect peace, whose mind is stayed on thee: because he trusteth in thee" (Isaiah 26:3). The word of God is the source book for getting our minds straight. Through nurturing our hearts with His precepts, our minds will be set on things above.

FOR THOUGHT AND DISCUSSION

1. Why has man been fascinated with the human mind?

2. How much "deep" thinking do you do each day?

3. Take 10 seconds and concentrate on ONE thing. Discuss in class.

4. Why does TV have such an influence upon viewers?

5. Why do we make so many decisions by impulses?

6. What are three major reasons why we don't take time to think?

7. Discuss Romans 8:6.

8. What do these verses mean?
   a. Proverbs 6:18.
   b. Ezekiel 8:12.
   c. II Corinthians 10:5.

9. What does it mean to be a "doubleminded man?" (cf. James 1:8).

10. What do you plan to do with the truths learned in this lesson?

11. Share 2 major applications of this lesson.

12. Discuss sowing and reaping.

CHAPTER NINE

YOU MUST KEEP IN MEMORY

What do you think about quoting Scripture to the Devil? Is it a new thought for you? Have you done it? Do you know anyone who does it, or anyone who has done it? It may surprise some persons to learn that this is what Jesus did.

After fasting for forty days, at a time when He would be the most vulnerable, Christ was approached by Satan and offered many challenges and rewards if He would obey him (cf. Matthew 4:1-11). In response to the Devil, Jesus said, ". . .It is written, Man shall not live by bread alone, but by every word that proceedeth out of the mouth of God" (Matthew 4:4). The Son of God, who had the power to perform miracles, used the Word of God which was stored in His heart to win over the evil one in this time of testing.

There is a vital lesson in this example of Jesus quoting Scripture to the Devil for each Christian. It lets us know that we, too, must store the word of God in our hearts. This insures us of power to win over temptations. The apostle Paul said, "There hath no temptation taken you but such as is common to man: but God is faithful, who will not suffer you to be tempted above that ye are able; but will with every temptation also make a way to escape, that ye may be able to bear it" (I Corinthians 10:13). One major way of escape is through using the Word (cf. Hebrews 4:12; Ephesians 6:13-18).

How does a person store the Word in his heart? Through memorization of Scripture. I know for many persons this is a "dirty" word. I say this because of the reactions I have seen through the years when I've suggested memory work, or made memory verse assignments. For some reason these two words (i.e. memory work) turn people off in a hurry. This is tragic because of the importance of memorizing God's word. Memorizing Scripture helps Christians defeat the Devil with the "sword of the Spirit."

One of the most important keys, therefore, to living a positive Christian life is a memorization of Bible verses. This is how you program your mind with positive ammunition and thoughts for living a victorious life. By having the word in your conscious mind, you will be able to make proper decisions. The word stored in your heart helps you act and react in a Christ-like manner.

Let me get personal for a minute. How much Scripture have you memorized? My observations in the brotherhood have led me to conclude that we aren't a Bible memorizing people. Sure there are a few exceptions to this. A few preachers and members of the church have spent long hours in memorizing God's word. How many verses can YOU quote from memory? I hope you don't answer this like one brother did. He replied, "Why should I memorize verses when I have a copy of the Bible. I can find verses when I *need* them."

This brother obviously didn't understand the deeper reasons for memorizing God's word. It is not, as some seem to think, to show off your ability, or to appear as a know-it-all; it is not an advocating of replacing the printed word. It is merely emphasizing the importance of doing what Jesus did. It is an attempt to prepare our minds with power to defeat the evil one. You can't live a positive Christian life without God's word. And the best place to have God's word is in your heart.

WHY MEMORIZE SCRIPTURE?

Since there are many misunderstandings about the importance and essentialness of memory work, as well as a lack of practicing it, it is necessary to notice some valid reasons for memorizing God's word.

First, because we love the word. Our attitude must be like the Psalmist of old, when he said, "I will delight in thy statutes: I will not forget they word" (Psalm 119:16). In Psalm 119:97 he said, "O how love I thy law!. . ." We put forth effort to remember names, places, things, dates, etc. that are important to us; how much more so the word of God. Do you love God's word enough to memorize it? _____ Yes _____ No

Second, because we must be ready. Peter said, "But sanctify in your hearts Christ as Lord: being ready always to give answer to every man that asketh you a reason concerning the hope that is in you. . ." (I Peter 3:15). Many times the need for answers will come when we do not have our Bible with us. Because you have memorized verses, you may be able to give answers right on the spot.

Third, because it will KEEP you from sin. Again, the Psalmist is our example when he said, "Thy word have I laid up in my heart, that I might not sin against thee" (Psalm 119:11). If we have the word in our hearts, it will help us recognize Satan's traps and, therefore, we can resist him. This is why we must arm ourselves with the word of God (cf. Ephesians 6:10-20). You will have a difficult time in thinking of sin and God's word at one and the same time.

Fourth, because it will help us maintain our salvation. Paul said, "Moreover, brethren, I declared unto you the gospel which I preached unto you, which also ye have received, and wherein ye stand; by which also ye are saved, if ye keep in MEMORY what I preached unto you. . ." (I Corinthians 15:1, 2). James reminds us that DOING the word will help us keep our souls saved (cf. James 1:21). This is why, therefore, that we must not be forgetful hearers (cf. James 1:25).

Fifth, because it will give you confidence. This confidence will also give you freedom in living the Christian life (cf. John 8:36). You will also have more confidence when you are teaching people. You will not spend so much time searching for the verses; neither will you, as a teacher, be glued to your notes or outline when you teach or preach. Nothing gives confidence like knowing God's word.

Sixth, because of the discipline. It takes hard work, as we shall see in a moment, to memorize Scripture. Many people avoid perpetual memory work because they do not like to work; they are not willing to pay the price, or discipline themselves to do it. Anything worth doing takes time and work. Memory work is no exception.

Seventh, because it will influence others. Many persons have been motivated to begin memory work programs because they hear a Scripture quoting preacher or Bible class teacher. I know in my case I was inspired by Johnny Ramsey, a teacher of mine, to memorize Scripture. We should want to encourage others to memorize God's word. We must not, however, confuse this with pride or showing off! This would be wrong and out of place for the child of God.

Eighth, because it will help preserve the word. F. S. Donnelson tells a story about 200 Chinese believers who memorized the entire New Testament because of their fear that Communism would destroy all the Bibles. They knew the word in their hearts couldn't be destroyed. I know several preachers today who could get together and reproduce the New Testament from memory. May their tribe increase!

Ninth, because it will help you break bad habits. I know a man who obeyed the gospel who was bound by the cursing habit. It didn't leave him when he came up from the baptistry. After weeks he still had the habit. Soon he began to doubt his conversion. After a while he got up enough nerve to tell his problem to the local preacher. The preacher told him about programming his mind with specific verses to combat vulgar language. By using such verses as Colossians 3:8 this new Christian was able to defeat the habit in three weeks. He was able to win the victory through thinking on the passages all through the day. It will work with any problem. Take the problem and find the verse that handles it. Place it in your memory and meditate on it all day and it will help you win over the problem.

Tenth, because it is good sowing. The mind is like the soil for a garden. Into it we plant seeds—either good or bad. The seed we must plant is the word of God (cf. Luke 8:11); by doing this we will reap a good harvest (cf. Galatians 5:5-8). The word of God is the BEST thing to put into your mind. It will help you act as Jesus acted. It will help you live a positive Christian life.

EXCUSES

Many persons upon being asked to memorize Scripture, reply with such statements as, "Oh, I just can't memorize," or "I forget so easily," or "I have a bad memory," and a host of other excuses.

A brief thought about such excuses will reveal that they, basically, are not true. These same people have memorized hundreds of things. In fact, our whole learning process is based upon memory. People memorize their name, the names of others, addresses, phone numbers, dates, directions, facts, etc. Why can't they memorize God's word? They can if they really want to.

What many persons fail to realize is that memorizing Scripture is done in much the same way as memorizing any other information. It takes desire, discipline, work, persistance and devotion to memorize God's word. You must throw aside "I can't" from your vocabulary. Remove all excuses by prayerfully committing yourself to memorizing God's word on a regular basis. Will you? ___Yes ___No. The choice is yours. The time is NOW!

KEYS TO MEMORIZING SCRIPTURE

First, there must be a positive interest and desire to do so. To approach memory work in a half-hearted way is to ensure failure. After a few attempts, without a deep desire, you will throw up your hands and say, "I can't do it."

Second, you must be motivated. All of the points discussed above, along with others, should provide proper motivation for memorizing Scripture. Look at it from the negative standpoint. Why shouldn't you memorize Scripture?

Third, you must give memory work your undivided attention. After you set aside a time period for memory work, do not let anything or anyone get your attention or turn you aside from your goal. Also, don't let daydreaming or other thoughts take control of your mind while you are doing your memory work. Give it your undivided attention.

Fourth, organize a systematic approach. Many become discouraged because they are trying to follow the "jump around" method of memorizing Scripture. You should memorize Scriptures that relate to a specific heading or the context of a book. For example, in the beginning you may want to memorize the key passage in the plan of salvation. Other good headings are: love, blood, worship, stewardship, etc. This helps you relate to a definite heading or key word.

It is based on the key of association.

Fifth, observe the context of the verse. Read it several times. If you do not understand the context, the verse may not have much meaning. By learning it in its context, you have something to relate it to; therefore, it will be easier to remember.

Sixth, try to visualize the scene or setting. This, also, is using the key of association. For example, Acts 17:20-31 stays in your mind as you visualize altars, philosophers, Paul, etc. Try to "see" your memory verses.

Seventh, try to associate the passage with others that you already know. This is closely akin to relating it to a topical heading. You may associate it with facts, special needs, certain conditions, etc., also.

Eighth, use repetition, repetition, repetition. After you have selected the portion to be memorized and followed the above points, the real work now begins. You must go over and over the verse. A good approach is to memorize a verse in the following way:

Romans 1:14

"I am a debtor both to the Greeks, and to the
Barbarians; both to the wise and to the unwise."

1. Repeat the following phrase 10 times: "I am a debtor both to the Greeks. . ."

2. Next repeat 10 times the next phrase: "And to the Barbarians. . ."

3. Then before you go on to the next phrase, go back and add, "I am debtor both to the Greeks", "and to the Barbarians", and repeat both 10 times without looking at your Bible. If possible, in the early stages of your work, say the verse out loud.

4. After this, repeat the next phrase: "both to the wise and to the unwise", 10 times. After this, repeat the entire verse 10 times without looking at your Bible.

Follow this procedure for five days. The verse should now be yours. You may memorize as many verses in a week as you so desire with this method. Just think, if you only do five per week, in one year that will be 260 verses, or 2600 in ten years. One additional word: you may also write out the verse using the above approach, or use a combination of verbal and writing. In either case, the

65

key to remembering is repetition, repetition, repetition, etc. There is no magical shortcut!

Ninth, try to use, as often as possible, every verse that you memorize. This will help you retain it. Also, think about it as you drive, cut the grass, play golf, etc. This is a good way to review your memory work. Use it, or lose it! If you use it, you won't lost it. Also, try to set aside a definite time for reviewing all of your memory work.

Tenth, prepare memory work cards. Any local printer will sell you a box of business card stock, or you may buy 3 x 5 cards at the local 5 & 10. On one side of the card, write or type the verse you want to memorize; and on the other side, write the book, chapter and verse location. Note the following example:

```
+-------------------------------------------+
|              Front of Card                |
|                                           |
|   I am debtor both to the Greeks,         |
|   and to the Barbarians; both to          |
|   the wise and to the unwise.             |
+-------------------------------------------+
```

```
+-------------------------------------------+
|              Back of Card                 |
|                                           |
|              Romans 1:14                  |
+-------------------------------------------+
```

You may carry these cards for study and review during the day as you have opportunity. For example, a good drill is to take your cards and look at the side with the book, chapter and verse, and quote the passage - then reverse the approach.

Eleventh, form a memory group, or choose a memory work partner. This will provide an extra incentive for memorizing God's word. It also helps you to say it in the presence of another person.

Twelfth, record the verse on a cassette tape. Listen to it while driving, working, before going to sleep, etc.

May God help us to dedicate ourselves to a memorizing of His word. Why not start today!

FOR THOUGHT AND DISCUSSION

1. How did Jesus defeat the Devil?

2. Who has a good command of memorized Scriptures (a person you know)?

3. Do you have a plan for memorizing the word?

4. Discuss organizing a "memory club" in your congregation.

5. Which verses would you tell a person to memorize if he has a cursing problem?

6. What is your greatest problem in memorizing Scripture?

7. Discuss the points related to WHY we should memorize Scripture.

8. Discuss some memory work books or courses you have heard about.

9. Why should we train children in memorizing Scripture?

10. What do you plan to do with the material in this lesson?

CHAPTER TEN

LOOK ON THE BRIGHTER SIDE

For a moment I want you to look at two situations with me. The first is that of a man in a restaurant with some friends. As he starts to take a bite of his spaghetti, sauce drips onto his shirt. This fellow goes into a rage. He not only upsets himself, but everyone around him, as he shouts, "My day is ruined! I won't be able to make my appointment..."

The next situation is also in a restaurant where a man is having lunch with some business acquaintances. As this man takes a bite of his potatoes, gravy drops onto his white shirt. This man smiles and says, "Oh well, I wanted a new white shirt anyway. After lunch I will go next door to the men's shop and buy myself a new one so that I can make my calls this afternoon."

In the above situations both men had frustrating experiences. The difference is in how they handled them. One man let the "little thing" get him down; while the other looked on the light side of the situation and was able to laugh at himself. Ethel Barrymore rightly said, "You grow up the day you have your first real laugh–at yourself."

Did you hear about the man who wanted to build two houses, one on each side of the street? This fellow always wanted the sun to shine on his front porch. I wonder what he did during the night?

I think most of us feel like this man in an emotional sense. We want the brighter side of life. We desire to bask in the "sunshine" of good times.

When I was a boy, my mother always told me to walk on the left side of the street when going to school. This was the side the sun shone on in the morning. Life always has its warm side, too, if we will look for it. Which side are you walking on?

It is not always easy to walk on the sunny side of the street of life. Try as we may, we find ourselves in the shadows and even in darkness (cf. Psalm 23).

All around us is the evidence that people are looking for the brighter side. "You Light Up My Life" was a popular song which expressed the need/want of most persons in search of the right person to brighten their lives. Everyone wants someone to whom he/she can sing, "You Are My Sunshine." An old song expresses it this way:

> "Keep on the sunny side,
> always on the sunny side,
> keep on the sunny side of life"

The TV news reporter who recently said, "Now for the brighter side of the news," was now to the news most persons were waiting to hear. When my son was six, he said, "Daddy, I don't like to hear the news because it is always bad." Thousands share my son's view. Sometimes we must search for the brighter side.

What is meant by the expression, "look on the brighter side"? The brighter side is *a way of looking* at the daily occurrences of life and passing a judgment on them. It is an attitude that looks for the other (i.e., brighter) side of every negative or bad thing that happens. Every dark situation, as far as the Christian is concerned, has a brighter side. The challenge is to find it.

A young man I know lost both his feet as the result of an accident. He went through some painful and frustrating days and nights as he sought to overcome his feelings of uselessness. With God's help he overcame this tragedy by looking on the brighter side. One day when we were discussing his past struggles, he said with a smile on his face, "I didn't lose my mind in the accident, and the weeks in the hospital brought me closer to God. I have so much to be thankful for, and I want to serve God more now than ever." What a great attitude! This positive attitude has helped this brother in Christ to reach the point where he is now "jogging" on his artificial limbs, and fulfilling his desire to serve God in a local church. The brighter side is real if we will look for it. It is as close as your next thought. (cf. Proverbs 23:7).

If you are a student of the Bible you probably have a set of commentaries by Matthew Henry, the famous scholar. There is an incident in his life that also illustrates our point.

On one occasion Henry was accosted and robbed by thieves. After the incident he wrote these words in his diary: "Let me be thankful first because I was never robbed before; second, although they took my purse, they did not take my life; third, because, although they took my all, it was not much; and fourth, because it was I who was robbed, not I who robbed."

The brighter side is there if you will prayerfully look for it. And remember when you look on the brighter side, you are living as God intended. Thus, come on out of the shadows into the sunshine of His love and mercy.

THE BRIGHTER SIDE IS BIBLICAL

The major reason why I believe looking on the brighter side is sound, workable advice is because it is based upon biblical principles.

In Job 14:1 we are reminded of the complexities of life: "Man that is born of a woman is of few days and full of trouble."

How are we to handle these troubles when they come? How is it possible to lift the dark clouds when they are trying to settle over our heads?

James tells us how to handle these challenges: "My brethren, count it ALL JOY when ye fall into manifold temptations; knowing this, that the trying of your faith worketh patience" (James 1:2, 3).

The average man on the street does not view "trials" as joy. In fact, this is the last thing he will probably think of doing when oppressions and hardships come his way. Thus, there are two ways to view the daily trials of life: (1) count them all joy; or (2) count them all tragedy; also, one may try to fool himself about trials and hope they will go away.

The word *count,* as used by James in our text, means to "deem it, consider, place a value on; weigh in a balance." After you have given deliberate and careful consideration to a thing (i.e., money, measure of wheat, or any other object, etc.) you are then able, based upon facts, to render a just appraisal or judgment as to its VALUE. In the area of daily trials, therefore, if we properly understand their value and benefit, we will count them (trials) all JOY.

The word JOY means to be delighted or pleased with something. In this case trials because of the great value. In the midst of ANY situation, the Christian has a "joy that is unspeakable" (I Peter 1:18).

James states we must count trials as joy because they help us become more patient, and as we are more patient we become more mature in the Lord (v. 3). These two qualities are musts if we desire to please God.

In the book of Romans the apostle Paul reminds us of the outcome of everything that happens to us: "And we know that all things work together for good to them that love God, to them who are called according to his purpose" (Romans 8:28).

Don't make the mistake of thinking that Paul is saying that EVERYTHING that happens to us *is good,* he is not. He is saying that everything that happens to us *will work for our good.* When the challenge comes we may not understand HOW it can bring about something good into our lives, but we must believe it and trust God to keep His promise to bring it about.

What's the worst thing that can happen to man? Death is the most frequent answer to this question. For the Christian there is even a brighter side to this stinging fate of all men (cf. Hebrews 9:27). The brighter side is seen in these biblical truths:

1. "Precious in the sight of the Lord is the death of his saints" (Psalm 116:15).

2. "Better is the day of death than the day of one's birth" (Ecclesiastes 7:1).

3. "Blessed are they that die in the Lord" (Revelation 14:13).

4. "To live is Christ, and to die is gain" (Philippians 1:21).

5. "The righteous have hope in death" (Proverbs 14:32).

6. ". . .depart and be with Christ" (Philippians 1:23).

7. "Precious in the sight of the Lord is the death of His saints.

There are many additional biblical truths that should be considered in our quest for power to live on the brighter side of life. Study carefully the following 15 truths that will help us look on the brighter side:

1. We must look through the eyes of faith (Hebrews 11:1). This will help us to see beyond the temporal and physical. Faith is an anchor for the soul.

2. We must learn the fine art of living one day at a time (Matthew 5:34). Trying to go back to yesterday is not possible, and we don't have tomorrow promised. This is the first day of the rest of your life.

3. Develop a positive way of thinking. (Proverbs 23:7). You are what you think! Negative thinking will destroy your desire and ability to look on the brighter side.

4. Trust God no matter what happens to you (Ephesians 3:20). There will be times when you will ask, "Why?" But don't let this hinder you from looking on the brighter side.

5. Do something positive (cf. James 1:18-21). Action makes things better. Work is one of the best therapies.

6. Live faithfully each day for the Lord (Revelation 2:10). This means to walk in the light in daily trust (cf. I John 1:7).

7. Find your purpose in life and live in harmony with it (cf. Revelation 4:11; Ecclesiastes 2:11, 17, 18).

8. Remember that God has placed you in the Light (Colossians 1:13), therefore, walk in it (I John 1:7).

9. Meditate on God's word on a daily basis (Psalm 119:48). There is power in this practice (Matthew 4:4).

10. Daily renew your mind (Ephesians 4:23). This is the key to victory.

11. Don't worry (Matthew 5:25-34). This destroys your peace of mind. In every situation, no matter how bad it looks, say, "It probably won't happen."

12. Look outward and find some way to help others (James 1:27; Galatians 6:10). You *get* by giving ("More blessed to give. . .").

13. Pray for wisdom (James 1:5). God promises to give us this great asset for living the good life.

14. Never forget this vital truth: "If God be for us, who can be against us." (Romans 8:31-35). You can't lose with God on your side.

15. Never forget that God loves *you* (John 3:16). This is why you are able to look on the brighter side.

16. In every adverse circumstance say: "This too shall pass." Even the darkest night is followed by a bright day. (Read the book of Job).

17. Count your blessings; it may surprise you how many you have.

PRACTICAL APPLICATION

There's always a brighter side. The challenge is to believe this and always look for it, and once you find it, accept it. *In every situation* ask yourself these questions:

1. What is the brighter side of this?
2. How can I get on the brighter side?

In every situation remember these two truths:

1. This too shall pass.
2. It probably won't happen.

To assist in finding the brighter side take a piece of paper and divide it into two columns by drawing a line down the center of it. On the left side write down the problem; on the right side write down the brighter side. Note the following example.

Dark Side	Brighter Side
1. I didn't get a raise.	1. I still have my job (some don't).
2. My friend won't obey the gospel.	2. She is alive and I will prayerfully try again. God gives the increase.

Dark Side	Brighter Side
3. I made a D on my report card.	3. I have two more quarters to make a better grade.
4. I have a tumor.	4. It can be removed.
5. I am confined to the house.	5. I can "leave" via phone, letters, books, TV, etc.
6. I missed my plane.	6. I'll have a few extra hours at home.

There was a blind man standing on the corner asking for money with this sign on his chest: "The sun is shining but I can't see it." This is always true in life – the sun is shining -- but you won't see it if you are closing your eyes to the brighter side. Open your eyes and live! Do it today by looking on the brighter side.

FOR THOUGHT AND DISCUSSION

1. Look up the definition of optimism.
2. Share a good illustration of a person (or yourself) looking on the brighter side.
3. Why do some persons always look for the darker side of things?
4. Who is the most optimistic person you know?
5. What would you tell a young man who just lost his girlfriend?
6. How do some people reject the idea of looking on the brighter side?
7. Can you think of a situation that doesn't have a brighter side?
8. Have you ever tried to go a day without saying something negative? Discuss.
9. What is your formula for looking on the brighter side?
10. How do you plan to use this lesson in your daily life?

CHAPTER ELEVEN

WINNING OVER WORRY

One Sunday morning I announced to the congregation that in the evening service I would be speaking on the subject of worry. Later, after services were dismissed, as I was visiting with persons in the foyer, a lady came up and informed me that she wouldn't be coming back that night. When I asked her why, she replied, "Well, worry is about all I have left to do, and it appears that you are taking that away from me."

This incident would be humorous if it wasn't for the fact that it describes how many persons give themselves to worry. Worry is a major enemy to positive Christian living. It robs a person of joy and peace of mind. It saps energy from your spiritual veins. It bitters your taste buds. It is a foe which causes you to toss and turn at night. We must defeat it or it will defeat us. The choice is ours.

WHAT IS WORRY?

Worry is an interesting word. The term (worry) comes from an Anglo-Saxon word meaning "to choke." The Greek word is *merimnao* which means "to be full of anxiety which divides up and distracts the mind; to be full of cares; anxious" (cf. Matthew 6:25, 27, 28, 31, 34; 10:19, Luke 12:11, 22, 26). Worry, then, is an emotional state of mind which chokes you physically and spiritually. It divides your emotions and leaves you without stability. It impairs your judgment and leaves you void of the ability to make sound decisions. Even your convictions are shallow and warped because of worry. Worry causes your imagination to run wild; it sees things all out of proportion. Worry can paralyze a person and keep him from taking constructive steps toward his goals and other ventures in daily living.

The expression, "You are going to worry yourself to death," has more truth in it than we may care to admit. I once heard of a person who could turn her asthma on and off by turning worry on and off. Also, it has been noted that a chronic worrier develops a smaller chest from failure to breathe deeply; he is afraid to take a deep breath. It has been estimated that 25 percent of all deaths of men over fifty are due to hypertension. Thus worriers seem to die before non-worriers. Worry, therefore, is deadly.

One has but to take a casual look into the face of his fellow man and he will see the signs of worry. It furrows the brows of millions like the ground left by a deep turning plow. An unknown author said, "Worry is an old man with bended head, carrying a load of feathers which he thinks are lead."

What is worry? According to Jesus it is a sin. This may sound a bit strong in light of all the worrying we do, but it is true. In Matthew 6:25, Jesus commanded us not to worry. He repeated the command in verses 31 and 34 of this chapter. I have always believed that to disobey Jesus was a sin. Hence, disobedience to the commands not to worry is wrong.

A closer look at some of the commands of Jesus will reveal a number of things He doesn't want us to worry about or be anxious over. Some of these are as follows:

1. Don't worry about your body being killed (cf. Matthew 10:28).

2. Don't worry about what you shall say during times of persecution (Mark 13:11 NIV).

3. Don't worry about building larger barns (warehouses) (Luke 12:16-21).

4. Don't worry about your life (Matthew 6:25 NIV).

5. Don't worry about what you shall eat or drink (Matthew 6:25 NIV).

6. Don't worry about clothes (Matthew 6:25 NIV).

7. Don't worry about tomorrow (Matthew 6:34 NIV).

The apostle Paul wrote, "Do not be anxious about anything, but in everything, by prayer and petition, with thanksgiving, present your request to God. And the peace of God, which transcends all understanding, will guard your hearts and your minds in Christ Jesus" (Philippians 4:6, 7). Paul is very positive: DO NOT BE ANXIOUS. This leaves no doubt about it being wrong for a Christian to worry.

In summary we have learned that worry is a destructive emotion that develops within the chambers of our minds. It is an emotion that causes us to violate the commandments of God. Worry is our enemy!

KEYS TO DEFEATING WORRY

COMMON SENSE KEYS:
There are a number of common sense solutions to worry if we will but use them. Some of the good ones are as follows:

First, a person must admit that he has a problem with worry. When you do this, you are on your way to winning over it.

Second, try to identify the source of your worry. Remember that it comes from WITHIN your mind. It is not an external force that breaks into your mind.

Third, if you don't intend doing something about it, worry is silly. If you intend to do something, worry isn't necessary.

Fourth, if you worry about what people think of you, it shows that you have more confidence in their opinions than you have in your own. The opinions of others have no power over you.

Fifth, remember this statistic: 90 percent of the things we worry about probably won't happen; 5 percent of the things we worry about can be helped if we will do something; that leaves only 5 percent that may happen. God has promised that even these things will work for our good (cf. Romans 8:28).

Sixth, ask yourself this question, "What is the worse possible thing that could happen in this situation?" No matter what it is, God will see you through.

Seventh, when you are prone to worry about something bad that may happen, tell yourself, "It probably won't happen." Say this over and over to yourself. It usually proves to be true.

Eighth, get a sheet of paper and fully evaluate the thing you are trying to keep from worrying about. Ask yourself, "Why am I worrying about this?" Then list all of the possible solutions to the problem you can think of, then get up and do something.

Ninth, talk to someone about the thing that is causing you to worry. There is great help in sharing with a close friend in the Lord. Many times just talking about it will cause it to go away.

Tenth, get busy. The more free or idle time you have, the more time you have for your mind to run wild and lead you into the worry trap. Work is a proven cure for worry.

BIBLICAL KEYS:

The best solutions to winning over worry are contained in God's word. The Father who created us knows what we must do in order to defeat worry.

In the Sermon on the Mount we have one of the greatest set of keys ever given by the Master for winning over worry. Get your Bible and read Matthew 6:24-34. Let's take a few moments and examine these keys given by Jesus for defeating worry.

First, you must establish the priorities for your life. Jesus makes it very clear that you can't serve "two masters." A man will never have peace of mind as long as he tries to live in two worlds. His mind will always be worried with his lack of commitment, as he knows that he is not what he should be. God must be first; if He isn't you will never have complete peace of mind. Thus, to win over worry you must put the Lord first in all that you do. In Matthew 10:32-39, Jesus makes it clear again that nothing must come between you and God. This is why we must deny ourself and take up our cross and follow Him (cf. Matthew 16:24).

Second, you must realize what is important in life. Clothing, food, and shelter are all secondary. We must focus our attention and energies on what is important in life (cf. Matthew 6:33). If we waste our energies on the secondary things we won't have strength to face the major challenges when they come.

Don't panic. Things aren't ever as bad as they seem. Don't place importance on problems that you will laugh at tomorrow. Most things will look small in retrospect. Miguel De Unamuno, a Spanish philosopher (1864-1936), said, "I am not going to weep today about something I am going to laugh about tomorrow," How true. Just think for a minute how many things you are now able to look back upon and laugh at. But when the thing happened you thought the end of the world had come. We all sit and talk about "remember when?" Those things now don't seem very important.

Postpone passing judgment on things of the moment, serious or nonserious. In light of God's plan and providence you don't have enough facts concerning the outcome of any events of today. Don't worry! Realize what is really important in life.

Third, we must learn to trust God's knowledge. In Matthew 6:30, Jesus states that He (God) "knows." We have difficulty with the present–can't remember the past–and don't know anything about the future. God, however, is ALL KNOWING (cf. Psalm 139:1-13).

To help us remember that we can trust the knowledge of God, Jesus gives us four illustrations from science that should convince us of this truth. Study carefully the following outline of the verses:

1. Biology - Birds, verse 26.
    a. They have to eat all of the time to survive. To "eat like a bird" a 180 lb. man would have to eat 9 pounds a day to eat as much as a bird based upon weight ratio. The average man eats 3 pounds per day. Yet God provides all of this food.
    b. A Chickadee the size of a man's thumb, can keep its body temperature at 105 when it is 45.
    c. If God can take care of birds, He'll take care of you.
2. Physiology - height of man, verse 27.
    a. Who can add 12 inches to his height? No one. You cannot change your height. Your genes

set it; that's it.
  b. Thus, we must realize that there are some things that we cannot change or do anything about. They are just that way, or will happen. Trust God!
3. Botany - flowers, verse 28.
  a. Flowers of the field cannot move to get food, yet God provides for them.
  b. If God can take care of a non-moving plant, He can take care of you.
4. Geology - clothed fields with grass, verse 30.
  a. God changes the "dress of the earth" four times a year.
  b. If God will dress a rock or field, how about you?

Let's trust the knowledge of God, He knows what is best for us.

Fourth, you must learn to live one day at a time. This truth is stressed in verse 34 of our text. Many people are frustrated because they never learn this lesson. Jesus promises us strength to handle the problems of TODAY. But we try to go back to yesterday's problems, and import tomorrow's problems. This is a deadly practice that must be stopped if we hope to win over worry.

People are always worrying about what might happen tomorrow. "What if I loose my job?" or "What if I get cancer?" or "What if my daughter marries the wrong boy?" Stop this practice! Wait until a thing happens before you concern yourself over it. Don't get bogged down with "what ifs."

We need to learn the fine art of starting all over each morning. Leave yesterday behind. "Today is the first day of the rest of your life." Live it to the fullest. It is ALL that you have. Don't worry about the future. It will have its own challenges. Be content with NOW.

Are you worried? Try these keys given by Jesus. They will work. He desires that you come unto Him with all your burdens (cf. Matthew 11:28-30). Do it now!

"Said the robin to the sparrow,
    I should really like to know
Why these anxious human beings
    Rush about and worry so.

Said the sparrow to the robin,
    I think it must be
They have no Heavenly Father
    Such as cares for you and me."

Positive Christian living will become a reality in your life when you STOP worrying.

FOR THOUGHT AND DISCUSSION

1. What are the three major things people worry about?

2. Who is more prone to worry, a Christian or a non-Christian?

3. Why is worry so deadly?

4. What do you worry the most about?

5. What is your personal plan for winning over worry?

6. What would you tell a person who is always worrying?

7. Do some additional research on worry and bring the results to class.

8. Discuss some of the keys to winning over worry. Which are the best?

9. Why is worry a sin?

10. How do you plan to use the material in this lesson in your daily life?

CHAPTER TWELVE

HAPPINESS IS STILL POSSIBLE

At thirty she looked like a person of fifty. Her face showed the results of sleepless nights, immorality, and a five year bout with drugs. She had all the marks of a loser, and had tried to take her life several times. With tears running down her cheeks, she asked, "Why can't I be happy and have peace of mind like other people?"

"Why can't I be happy?" is a question raised by thousands like the lady mentioned above. Happiness, as a general rule, is the quest of all people. But in reality it is an elusive gem rarely found by the majority. "How may I be happy?" is the question all men seek a favorable answer to, as they look for the good life. The world is searching for peace and happiness.

Everywhere you look there are promises of happiness. A sign outside a bar reads, "Happy Hour from 5-6." One is caused to wonder about the other 23 hours in the day. Is happiness only possible for one hour each day? A 32 hour work week, with more time for recreation is suggested as a sure route to happiness. Get this, go there, do this, etc., are summaries of the hundreds of commercial appeals which bombard our minds weekly in an attempt to lead us to happiness. But, for some reason, man is still not happy.

Are you happy, really happy? What constitutes REAL happiness? Varro, a writer from the past, listed 280 different opinions of what constitutes happiness. Stop 12 persons on the street and ask them, "What constitutes happiness?" and you will probably get 12 different answers. This is true because most persons don't understand the true nature and source of happiness. Man will never be happy until he has the true answers to these two questions.

THE SEARCH FOR HAPPINESS

There is a story about eight men who were once taking a trip together; when each gave his reply to the question, "Are you happy, really happy?" A banker said he had acquired a fortune, which was invested beyond any possibility of loss; that he had the most lovely and devoted family, yet the thought that he must leave them forever cast a dark cloud over the decline of his life. A military officer said that he had known the glory of triumph; but after the battle, he passed over the field, and found a brother-officer dying. Trying to relieve him, the dying man said, "Thank you; but it is too late. We must all die: think about it; think about it." This scene and these words fastened upon him, and he couldn't find escape from them. He confessed his unhappiness. A diplomatist spoke of the honors and gratitude showered upon him during a long and successful career, yet confessed an emptiness of heart, a secret malady, which all his honors couldn't cure. A poet told of the pleasure he enjoyed with the Muses; of the applause of the people; of his fame, which he was assured was "immortal": but, dissatisfied, he cries out, "What is such an immortality?" and declares his unsatisfied longing for happiness and a higher immortality. A man of the world said that his efforts had been to laugh at everything; to look at the bright side of all things, and be gay; to find pleasure in the dance halls, movies, and other amusements; yet confessed that he wasn't happy. A lawyer seventy years old said that he had health, wealth, reputation, and domestic security; that, during his period of labor, he longed for just what he now possessed; but he did not find the expected enjoyment, and contentment was not his heritage. His hours were long; his existence monotonous; he was not fully happy. A professor of religion, who seemed to have been only a ritualist at best, professed his strict adherence to the doctrines of the Bible, and his punctual performance of its duties, without being happy. A physician narrated his search for happiness in the world and in his profession in vain; how he had been led by the Scriptures to see himself as a sinner, and to look to Christ as his Saviour: since which he had found peace, contentment, and joy, and had no fear to the end, which to him was but the beginning of real happiness.

This brief story covers most of the major ways people believe happiness comes. Yet, according to seven of these men, the roads are only dead end streets. Like Solomon, these men searched for ways to cheer their flesh (cf. Ecclesiastes 2:3), but to no satisfaction. In essence they reached the same conclusion Solomon reached; "I have seen all the works that are under the sun; and, behold, all is vanity and a striving after wind" (Ecclesiastes 1:14). From this it becomes apparent that happiness must come some other way.

WHAT IS HAPPINESS?

What comes to your mind when you think of happiness? How would you define the word? Webster defines happiness, a noun form of happy, as "a feeling of great pleasure, contentment, glad, pleased." The Greek word for "happy" (or blessed KJV) is *makarios*. This word was originally used to describe the condition of the gods as opposed to the condition of men. In Christianity it was used to describe the spiritual position which men enjoyed through Christ. It is, as Peter stated, "a joy unspeakable."

Kant, the philosopher said, "Real happiness rests with my free volition, and real contentment consists in the consciousness of freedom."

Happiness is an inner state of being. It is a peace that passeth all understanding. It is a calmness and assurance given ONLY by God and His word. He comes from being right with God (cf. Matthew 5:1-12). The wise man said, "He that giveth heed unto the word shall find good; and whoso trusteth in Jehovah, happy is he" (Proverbs 16:20). "Happy is he that hath the God of Jacob for his help. . ." (Psalm 146:5). Happiness is from God. This is why, therefore, it is still possible.

WHY PERSONS AREN'T REALLY HAPPY

We have already noticed that most persons aren't happy because they are searching in the wrong places. To this I would like to list some additional major reasons why persons aren't happy.

1. People aren't happy because their lives aren't right with God. Solomon, who tried everything in his search for happiness, said, "Let us hear the conclusion of the whole matter: Fear God, and keep His commandments: for

this is the whole duty of man" (Ecclesiastes 12:13). This is why Jesus came to give life to all who will obey Him (cf. John 10:10, Hebrews 5:8, 9). If you aren't really happy, take time to check your relationship with God.

2. Some people aren't happy because things don't go their way. Many are like king Ahab who wanted what he couldn't have (cf. I Kings 20). Happiness comes through being content with such things as you have. Read the book of Ecclesiastes.

3. Scores of people aren't happy because they have minds full of guilt. The classic example of this state is seen in Judas who sold the Lord for thirty pieces of silver. Later, when he remembered his sin, he committed suicide. The blood of Christ forgives sins (cf. Matthew 26:28), this is why the Christ is able to defeat guilt.

4. People aren't happy because they have a poor opinion of themselves. A lack of self-love will rob you of peace and happiness. This is why Jesus said, "Thou shall love thy neighbor as thyself." The basis of self-love is the truth that we are created in God's image (cf. Genesis 1:27).

5. Happiness eludes many because they fail to understand the source of happiness. There are three truths relative to this point: (1) God is the giver of true happiness; (2) The Bible is the guide book to happiness; and (3) the mind of man is the chooser of happiness. Abraham Lincoln rightly said, "I have found that most people are about as happy as they make up their minds to be." God and His word have done their part, it is now up to man to choose. "What you demand," wrote Horace, "is here. You compass the world in search of happiness, which is within the reach of every man: a contented mind confers it on all."

Man's attitude plays a major role in his quest for happiness. In fact, it determines how he will react to God and His word. Johnson states the importance of the mind in these words: "The fountain of content must spring up in the mind; and he who has so little knowledge of human nature as to seek happiness by changing anything but his own disposition, according to Jesus, begins by being poor in spirit" (cf. Matthew 5:1-12). Happiness is a choice. It doesn't depend upon circumstances. It depends upon the state of your mind. If you aren't happy, you may need to change your mind!

6. Many aren't happy because they are holding anger and resentment in their hearts. This is where the power of forgiveness comes to our aid. Jesus tells us that we must be willing to forgive seven times in one day (cf. Luke 17:1-7). A mind will not be at peace while it harbors these sins. Paul said, "Don't let the sun go down on your anger" (cf. Ephesians 4:26). If you hold anger, it will hold you.

7. Masses are unhappy because they don't know their purposes in life. Our major purposes are described in the Bible, and elsewhere in this book. We must learn these and seek to live in harmony with them. Let it be noted here that our major purpose is to bring pleasure to God (cf. Revelation 4:11). Are you doing this?

8. Happiness escapes many because they never learn the virtue of giving. Jesus said, "It is more blessed (happy) to give than to receive" (Acts 20:35). This is one of the major avenues of happiness. A person who gives his time, talent, and money for the good of another, will one day notice that he has a peace of mind that is beyond understanding. True happiness comes through giving to others. History confirms that the "keepers" have not been happy (e.g., Howard Hughes).

9. Another cause of unhappiness is a failure to seek God's will for our life. This is done through Bible study and prayer. James said, "For that ye ought to say, If the Lord will, we shall live, and do this, or that" (James 4:15). Many persons are unhappy because they know their life-styles are out of harmony with God's word. "To him therefore that knoweth to do good and doeth it not, to him it is sin" (James 4:17).

10. Unhappiness is the result of trying to carry your own burdens. Jesus said, "Come unto me, all ye that labour and are heavy laden, and I will give you rest. Take my yoke upon you, and learn of me; for I am meek and lowly in heart: and ye shall find rest unto your souls. For my yoke is easy, and my burden is light" (Matthew 11:28-30). Peter states it this way: "Humble yourselves therefore under the mighty hand of God, that he may exalt you in due time: Casting all your care upon Him; for He careth for you" (I Peter 5:6, 7). From these verses we learn that Jesus not

only handles our sin problem, He also helps us handle the daily burdens of life (cf. Matthew 6:34). The key is to turn them over to HIM.

No doubt there are many other reasons why people aren't happy. The ten we have noticed, however, constitute some of the major reasons for unhappiness. Take a moment and see if you can think of some additional ones. Also remember the opposite of these will bring happiness. Take a few minutes and think about this.

The Constitution of the United States guarantees each citizen the right to the pursuit of happiness. This guarantee, however, doesn't include the ability to catch it. This ability comes from a positive relationship with God. It is in the heart, not in the circumstances. An effort made for the happiness of OTHERS lifts us above ourselves. Happiness isn't so much a matter of position as it is of disposition. A disposition taught in Matthew 5:1-12 is the basis of TRUE and lasting happiness. Marcus Aurelius said, "The happiness of your life depends upon the character of your thoughts." We are brought back to the words of the wise man, "As a man thinketh in his heart, so is he" (Proverbs 23:7). Happiness is a state of mind. Someone has said, "If you have to take one step (i.e. physical step) to find happiness, you won't find it. It is within the heart." Take a moment and think about this statement.

It is not WHERE you are but WHAT you are that determines your happiness. Someone may ask, "What am I?" If you are a Christian, the answer is clear: *You are a child of the King.* As a child of the King, happiness is your birthright. It is up to you to claim it. The choice is yours. The time is NOW!

FOR THOUGHT AND DISCUSSION

1. Do you agree that most persons are looking for happiness? Why?

2. Share some specific examples of pseduo attempts to bring happiness.

3. What was the happiest period in your life?

4. Locate 5 verses in the Bible that deal with happiness.

5. Who is the happiest person you know? Why is he/she happy?

6. Discuss the meaning of the Beatitudes in Matthew 5:1-12.

7. What advice would you give an unhappy person?

8. How and why is happiness a state of mind?

9. How does helping others bring you happiness?

10. How do you plan to us this lesson in your daily life?

CHAPTER THIRTEEN

POSITIVE HABITS

"Habit," wrote Horace Mann, "is a cable; we weave a thread of it every day, and at last we cannot break it." A Czech Proverb says, "Habit is a shirt made of iron." Wildrooter said, "Habits don't have a hold on you—you have a hold on them."

Habits are powerful.

What is a habit? Webster defines it as "a characteristic condition of the mind or body; disposition. A thing done often, hence, easily."

Every person is the possessor of hundreds of habits. From the side of the bed we sleep on, to the route we drive to work, habits are constantly with us. Some of these habits are good, and some are bad. Some are known, and some are not known (i.e., little peculiar mannerisms). This is why it is important to take a few minutes and discuss the subject of habit.

If you desire to be successful, you must develop positive habits. Positive habits develop the winning personality, without which, you cannot succeed.

Positive habits bring happiness. Positive habits help you look on the brighter side.

Since personality is the center of success, we need to stress the basic habits that develop it. What is personality? It is a certain magnetic outward expression of the inner being which radiates confidence, courage, courtesy and leadership. It attracts people by producing a pleasing effect. It is the product of positive habits. Daily we hear this expression, "He sure has a good personality." This should be the goal of every person.

What are some of the positive habits we must develop and maintain if we expect to succeed in the affairs of life? Some that must be given priority are as follows:

First, we must develop the habit of positive thinking. The wise man said, "As a man thinketh in his heart, so is he" (Proverbs 23:7). It is a known fact that every idea which enters into the mind immediately tends to express itself in action. This is why we must develop the habit of thinking on things "true, honorable, just, lovely, of good report, virtuous, of praise" (Philippians 4:8). The choice is ours - the time is now!

Second, we must develop the habit of prayer. The young man Daniel is worthy of imitation (cf. Daniel 1, 2, 3). To develop this habit will require a specific plan that is worked on each day. We must never become too busy to pray.

Third, we must develop the habit of forgiveness. This is not easy, especially when you have been wronged. Jesus said to forgive 70 times 7. A good habit, therefore, would be to close each day by forgiving every person who has wronged you, or you have ought against. This will prevent accumulation, and helps us live one day at a time (cf. Matthew 6:34, 35).

Fourth, we must develop wholesome speech habits. Paul wrote, "Let your speech be always with grace, seasoned with salt, that ye may know how ye ought to answer each one" (Colossians 4:6). This is a lifetime challenge, which requires setting a "watch upon our lips" (Psalm 141: 3). The tongue is hard to control (cf. James 3:1-13).

Fifth, we must develop the habit of kindness. This must be demonstrated in actions and works. Paul wrote, "be ye kind one to another."

Sixth, we must develop the persistency habit. Jesus said, "No man having put his hand to the plow and looketh back is fit for the kingdom of God." This means that we must finish what we start. We must vow never to give up. Edison said genius is 99% perspiration and 1% inspiration. Work is a must!

Seventh, we must develop the habit of looking for the good in others. The tendency is to shop for flaws in the other person's character. Love doesn't do this. Paul wrote, ". . .love thinketh no evil. . ." (I Corinthians 13:4-7). Jesus said not to worry about the speck in the other person's eye when you have a log in yours.

Eighth, we must develop the balance habit. Life is not composed of one facet but many. Work must not consume all your time and energy; neither must play, etc. Balance is the key.

Ninth, we must develop the study habit. Some persons never read anything, much less the Bible or other good materials. The Bible says, "Study to show thyself approved unto God" (II Timothy 2:15). Study in all areas of your vocation. It will move you up the ladder of success.

Tenth, we must develop the cooperation habit. A number of years ago Harvard University studied 4,375 men who had failed and lost their jobs. It was discovered that 65.8% of them failed because of personality qualities. Heading the list of 14 destructive personality qualities was a failure to cooperate. In contrast only 34.2% failed because they lacked technical knowledge. Thus it is clear that personality, which is the product of habits, plays a key role in daily success and failures.

Eleventh, we must develop the habit of initiative. This is just the opposite of sitting and waiting for "George to do it." The person with initiative makes things happen; you don't have to lead him around "by the nose" and show him the next move. He is a planner and fulfiller of plans. This type doesn't have a lazy bone in his body. He is the fellow others resent because he is a DOER.

Twelfth, we must develop the habit of being thankful. "Thank you" are two of the hardest words in the English language for some persons to say. Many persons feel strange or awkward when they utter these two powerful words. The Bible says in "everything give thanks." Make a practice of saying "Thank you" on all occasions; even for the small things. It will make a difference. Try it!

Thirteenth, we need to develop the habit of considering new ideas. A famous educator and teacher on one occasion was asked what had impressed him the most during his 40 years of teaching and dealing with students. He replied, "It is the resistance of the human mind to new ideas." This is why you must not only welcome new ideas, but look for them on a daily basis. Success depends on them.

Fourteenth, we must develop the loyality habit. First, we must be loyal to our Creator; second, we must be loyal to others; and third, we must be loyal to ourselves. "To thy ownself be true" is some very good advice.

There are persons who spend their time running down the company they work for, or the persons they work with, etc. This never, never leads to success. Loyalty is a major need in our day.

Fifteenth, we must develop the habit of patience. This virtue is the ability to calmly stand up under the pressures of life without blowing your cool. James wrote that the daily trials of life help us develop patience, and patience helps us develop maturity (James 1:2-6). Stick-to-it-tiveness is another word for patience.

Sixteenth, we must develop the habit of responsibility. You are NOT responsible for everything that happens to you, but you are responsible for HOW you handle it. This is not very popular in our "pass the buck" age. We must believe in the responsibility of every person, as well as our responsibility. Our actions, outlooks, and all other character traits are personal responsibilities; we can't shift the blame for our failures in these areas to anyone else.

Seventeenth, we must develop the habit of answering all persons properly. When you shout—persons will shout back. "A soft answer turneth away wrath: but grievous words stir up anger" (Proverbs 18:13). Be sure you get all the facts before you answer; then be very careful.

Eighteenth, we must develop the habit of paying the other person a genuine compliment. This is a key to personal relations. It is true because every person needs to feel important. It will not be very difficult to find things to compliment the other person about. Just look!

Ninteenth, we must develop the habit of being friendly. The wise man said, "To have a friend, you must show yourself friendly." (Proverbs 18:24).

This list could go on and on. These 19 specific habits, that are positive in nature, should serve to launch you into a perpetual self-improvement program. The question is—HOW do you develop new habits? I believe the basic answer is found in Webster's definition of habit: "It is a characteristic condition of mind or body." This means that you must program your mind to develop a habit. You must think about it, and set down a plan of action for developing it.

Webster also said habit is "a thing done often." This means we must PRACTICE the desired habit. A beginning piano player is a good example. At first playing the scale is very difficult. After hours of practice, however, it can be played with the eyes closed. Why? Because of habit.

Psychologists tell us that it takes a minimum of 17 to 21 days to stabilize the seeds for a new habit. During the 21 days the habit must be constantly practiced and re-enforced.

FOR THOUGHT AND DISCUSSION

1. Why are habits so hard to break?
2. Share some additional good habits we need to develop.
3. Discuss how to best break the gossip habit.
4. Is the church going "habit" wrong or bad as some people are saying?
5. Share an illustration of a person you know who has broken a habit.
6. What would you tell a person who has the habit of wasting money?
7. Read something positive about habits and share it with the class.
8. Why is it difficult to realize all the bad habits we may have?
9. What is the most difficult thing about breaking a habit?
10. How do you plan to use this lesson in your daily life?

Other Helpful Books
By:
J. J. Turner

DOCTRINE OF THE GOD HEAD

This study of the Father, Son, and Holy Spirit by J.J. Turner and Edward P. Myers covers subjects such as The Attributes of God, The Triune Godhead, The Nature of God, and The Incarnation of Jesus. The Holy Spirit of God, of Today, and in the Testaments is also discussed.

HOW TO TURN YOUR DREAMS INTO REALITIES

This self-improvement book seeks to motivate you to go to work on making your dreams a reality. Some of the chapter titles are: "Whatever Happened To All The Great Things You Were Going To Do?", "It's Not Too Late," "Find A Way Or Make One," "30 Mistakes On The Road To Success," and "Unleashing Your Potential."

WINNING THROUGH A POSITIVE SPIRITUAL ATTITUDE

This book sets forth a sound biblical approach to being successful in ALL areas of life. It is fast becoming a best seller in the brotherhood as it is being used in special classes, as well as ladies Bible classes.

THE BOOK OF JAMES

This practical book is designed to give an understandable exegesis of the text with application for people of today.

GOD'S WAY TO THE TOP

We have a lot of advice today on how to get to the top, but it should be remembered that God also has some information on how to succeed and get to the top. This book is about that advice.

HOW TO WIN OVER EMOTIONS

A study of the very important role that emotions play in man's everyday life. The challenge for man is to recognize the valid place for good, healthy emotions in his life. He must control his emotions, which is possible through help from God.

These books may be ordered from
Quality Publications
P.O. Box 1060   or
Abilene, Texas 79604   your favorite bookstore.

DATE DUE

248
TUR TURNER, J.J.
POSITIVE CHRISTIAN
LIVING.